ISBN 2 87424 114 8

Legal deposit : June 2006

Printed in Belgium

Note to parents: adult supervision is recommended
when sharp-pointed items such as scissors are in use.

Conceived, designed and written by Guy Harvey and Simon Beecroft
in collaboration with studio Moulinsart

éditions ***moulinsart***

Contents

CLAC

Welcome

Adventures can begin in unexpected places. Just walking along a leafy lane, you never know what you'll see: a speeding car, a crashed plane, a message in code. To be a great detective like Tintin, you must always be alert. This book is full of puzzles and activities that will help you sharpen your senses, and one day – who knows – you might even solve a real-life mystery yourself!

Know Your Enemy

Tintin's world is full of deadly criminals. And when you are constantly followed by shadowy villains, it is important to recognise their terrible traits. Here is a rogue's gallery of the most villainous villains of all. Read and beware!

Rastapopoulos

First name: Roberto

Also known as: Marquis di Gorgonzola

Occupation: Master criminal, film tycoon

Nationality: Greek-American

Distinguishing features: Bald head, secret society tattoo on left arm, nose like a proboscis monkey

Characteristics: Ruthless, charming, short-tempered

Catchphrase: Diavolo! (Italian for "devil")

Mitsuhirato

Occupation: Spy, opium distributor, villain

Nationality: Japanese (living in China)

Distinguishing features: Round glasses, moustache, upturned nose, false smile

Characteristics: Devious, charming, easily enraged

Plans to kill Tintin: By injecting him with the drug of madness, then stabbing him with his knife

How Tintin escapes: By replacing the drug with water and swapping the knife for a tin one

Final act: Commits hara-kiri (ritual suicide) when exposed as a smuggler and spy

Bobby Smiles

Occupation: Gangland boss

Nationality: American

Distinguishing features: Big grin, round glasses, tall boots

Characteristics: Corrupt, smooth-talker, prefers to pay others to do his dirty deeds

Ends up: Tied up and posted in a box to the Chief of Police by Tintin!

Dr J. W. Müller

Also known as: Mull Pasha, Professor Smith

Official occupation: Director of a psychiatric clinic (in which his enemies are given a madness-inducing treatment)

Actual occupations: Member of gang of forgers (in *The Black Island*) ; secret agent plotting to destroy world fuel supplies (in *Land of Black Gold*) ; Sheik Bab El Ehr's military adviser (in *The Red Sea Sharks*)

Distinguishing features: Bald with whiskers (and later a full beard)

Characteristics: Wealthy, wicked

Catchphrases: Kruziturcken!; Ach!

Allan

Surname: Thompson

Occupation: First mate under Captain Haddock ; smuggler and henchman to Rastapopoulos

First appearance: Captain of the smuggling ship *Sereno* (in *Cigars of the Pharaoh*)

Distinguishing features: Sailor's cap, long face, big fists

Characteristics: Mocking, cruel, violent

Final fate: Apparently carried away by alien spaceship, along with his boss, Rastapopoulos

Colonel Sponsz

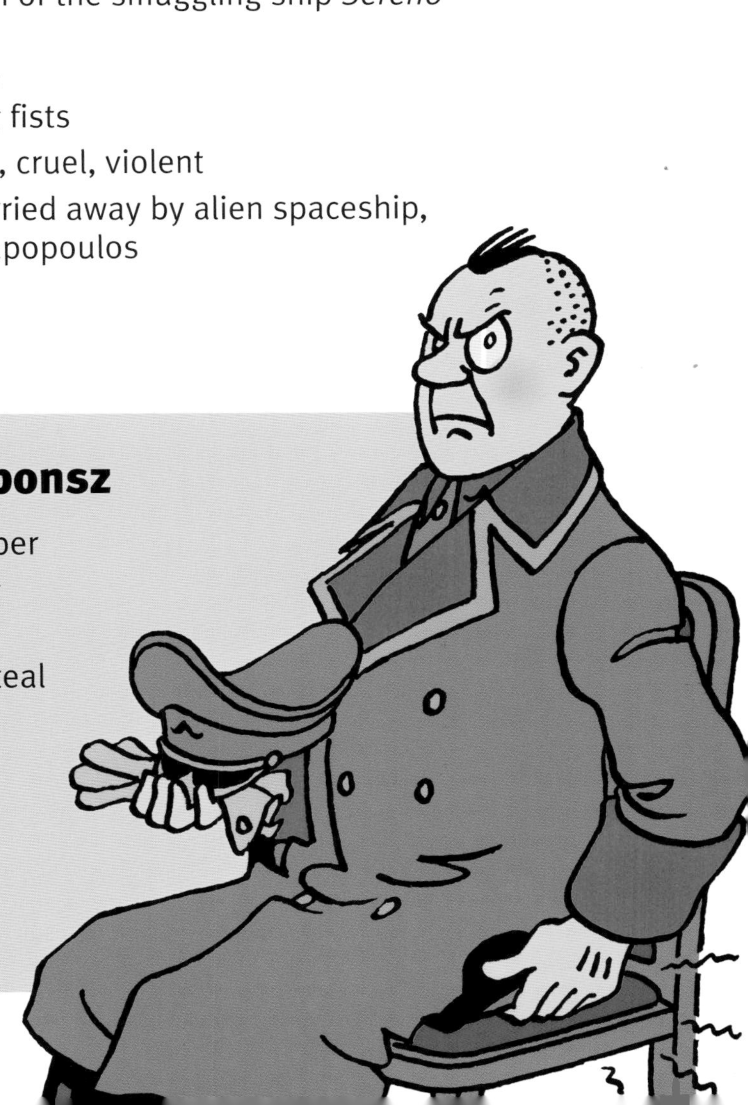

Occupation: Chief of Police in Borduria ; kidnapper

Also known as: Colonel Esponja, when advising General Tapioca (in *Tintin and the Picaros*)

Plots: To kidnap Cuthbert Calculus in order to steal the Professor's plans for an ultrasound weapon ; after he is discovered, he attempts to kill Tintin, Haddock and Calculus in revenge

Distinguishing features: stern expression, shaved head, monocle

Characteristics: fond of surveillance

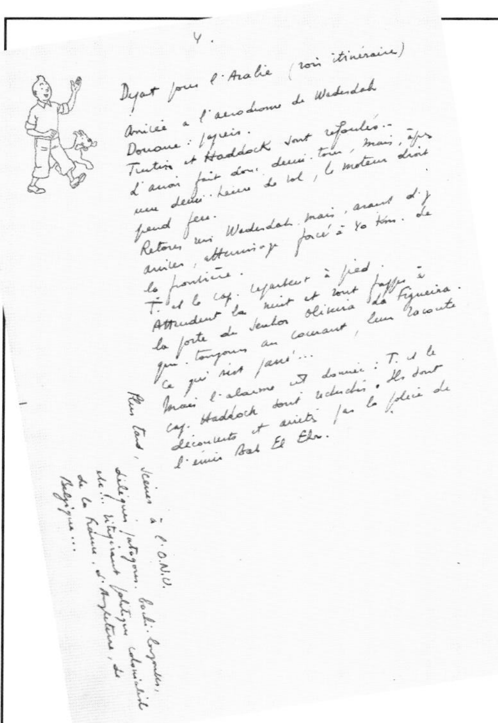

4.

Départ pour l'Arabie (voir itinéraire)

Arrivée à l'aérodrome de Wadesdah
Douane : papiers.
Tintin et Haddock sont refoulés.–
L'avion fait donc demi-tour, mais, après
une demi-heure de vol, le moteur droit
prend feu.
Retour vers Wadesdah mais, avant d'y
arriver, atterrissage forcé à 40 km. de
la frontière.
T. et le cap. repartent à pied.
Attendent la nuit et vont frapper à
la porte de Senhor Oliveira da Figueira.
qui, toujours au courant, leur raconte
ce qui s'est passé...
Mais l'alarme est donnée : T. et le
cap. Haddock sont recherchés. Ils sont
découverts et arrêtés par la police de
l'émir Bab El Ehr.

Plus tard, séance à l'O.N.U.
délégués patagons, [illegible]
etc... litiges politique coloniale
de la France, d'Angleterre, de
Belgique...

From Sketch to Print

All of Tintin's adventures were written and drawn by a talented artist who called himself Hergé (although his real name was Georges Remi). Each book took a long time to complete. So when you are next reading one, think about all the work that went into it!

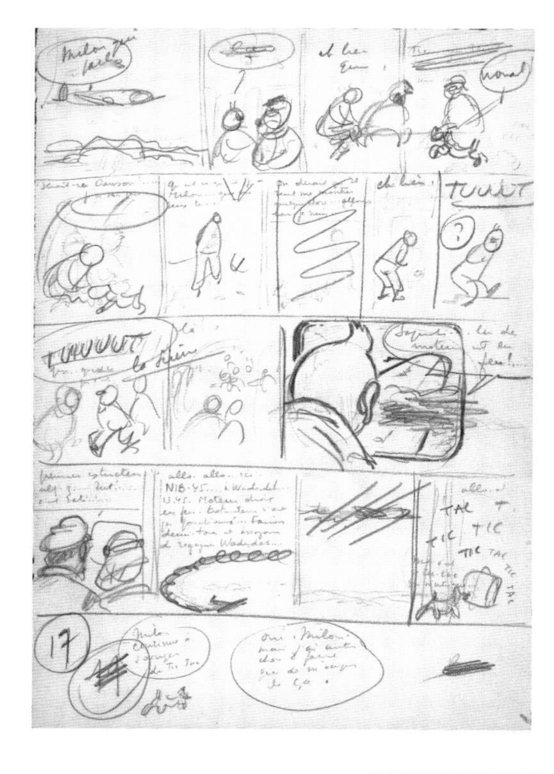

1 Rough Plan

When Hergé began work on a new story, he first wrote out a broad outline, called a synopsis. Sometimes, he illustrated the synopsis with a few sketches.

2 First Draft

When Hergé was happy with the rough story, he drew the whole story again more carefully. He researched all the tiny details to make the story look real.

3 Pencils

Then the story was drawn out again neatly in pencil. At this stage, Hergé carefully worked out how the words would fit with the pictures.

4 Inks

Next, Hergé would ink over the pencil drawings. He knew how much space he would need for the words, so he left blank speech boxes. The text would be added later.

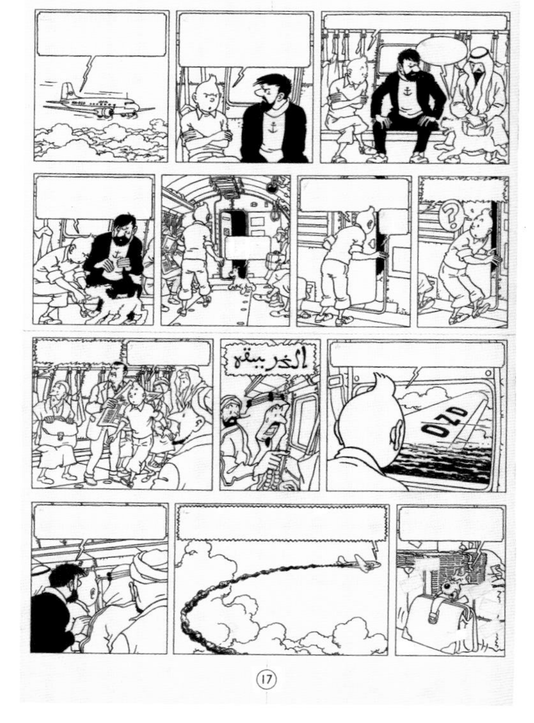

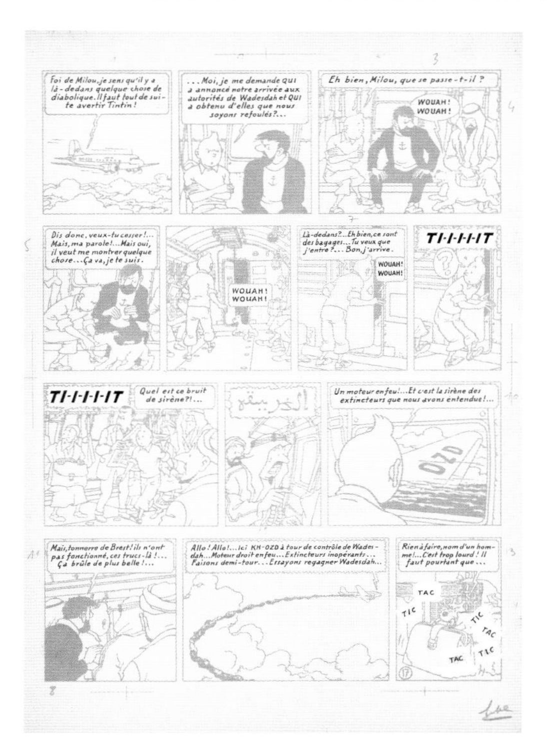

A black-and-white photograph of a page from *Flight 714 to Sydney*.

5 **Photographed Pages**

Hergé's inked pages were then sent to a special photography studio to be photographed. This way, they could be enlarged or reduced to fit the size of the pages in the actual book. A printed-out black-and-white copy of the photographed pages would then go to the colouring team.

6 **Colours**

The colourists placed see-through cellophane over the black-and-white pages. They painted on to the cellophane up to the black lines, but not over them – a very difficult, skilled job.

Each colourist would do a different colour – one would paint Tintin's hair, for example.

7 **Words**

The words were also carefully drawn on to a separate sheet from the drawings, so they could be translated. Every word is translated – even sneezes and other sounds.

8 **Printed Books**

All the pages could then go to the printer – the black-and-white pages, the colour pages and the pages with the words. The pages are printed and made into books. Since 1930, a Tintin book has been bought every 20 seconds somewhere in the world. That's a lot of books!

The Tintin Test

Four sections covering four aspects of Tintin's adventures – test yourself or quiz a friend... who knows the most?

(Answers on page 68)

A

Part 1 : Marlinspike Hall

B

1 Who owns Marlinspike before Haddock?

A Red Rackham
B The Bird Brothers
C Professor Calculus

2 Where is Red Rackham's treasure hidden?

A In a globe
B In a suit of armour
C In a statue of an eagle

3 How did Haddock buy back Marlinspike?

A With his sailor's pension
B With Red Rackham's treasure
C Calculus bought it for him when he sold his submarine

C

4 Which picture is NOT at Marlinspike?

D

Part 2 : Transport

1 What is the name of Haddock's ship?

A Karaboudjan
B Djebel Amilah
C Sirius

2 What is the final destination of Flight 714?

A Sydney, Australia
B Jakarta, Indonesia
C Pulau-pulau Bompa Island, Indonesia

3 How many times does Tintin drive a tank?

A Once
B Twice
C Three times

Part 3 : Great Escapes

1 How does Tintin escape from Marlinspike Hall's dungeons in *The Secret of the Unicorn* ?

A In a suit of armour
B With a battering ram
C With a halberd (pole weapon)

2 How does Tintin escape from Al Capone's gang in America ?

A The police rescue him
B He pretends he has a gun
C Snowy pushes a vase on to the gangster's head

3 What is at the end of the rope in this picture from *The Crab with the Golden Claws* ?

A Two large books
B Planks of wood
C A tin of crab

Part 4 : Tintin's Adventures

1 In which adventure does Tintin first meet General Alcazar ?

A *The Seven Crystal Balls*
B *Tintin and the Picaros*
C *The Broken Ear*

2 In which adventure does Tintin rescue Chang from the Yeti ?

A *The Red Sea Sharks*
B *Tintin in Tibet*
C *The Blue Lotus*

3 Which adventure is set in Scotland ?

A *The Shooting Star*
B *The Calculus Affair*
C *The Black Island*

4 In which of these pictures is Tintin NOT in South America ?

A

B

C

D

Unmask Tintin

Tintin has disguised himself as one of the Brotherhood. If this dangerous secret society find out that there is a spy in its midst, it will kill him! But which Brother is Tintin? Can you work it out from the statements below?

The sinister Brotherhood meet in a secret chamber.

Mrs Snowball sits two from the centre.

Mr Snowball sits on his wife's right; he is furthest away from Tintin.

On Mrs Snowball's left is the Colonel.

The Fakir is in between the Colonel and the Maharaja's secretary.

The Maharaja's secretary sits on the Fakir's left.

The Japanese man sits next to the Maharaja's secretary.

Which Brother is Tintin?

(Answer on page 68)

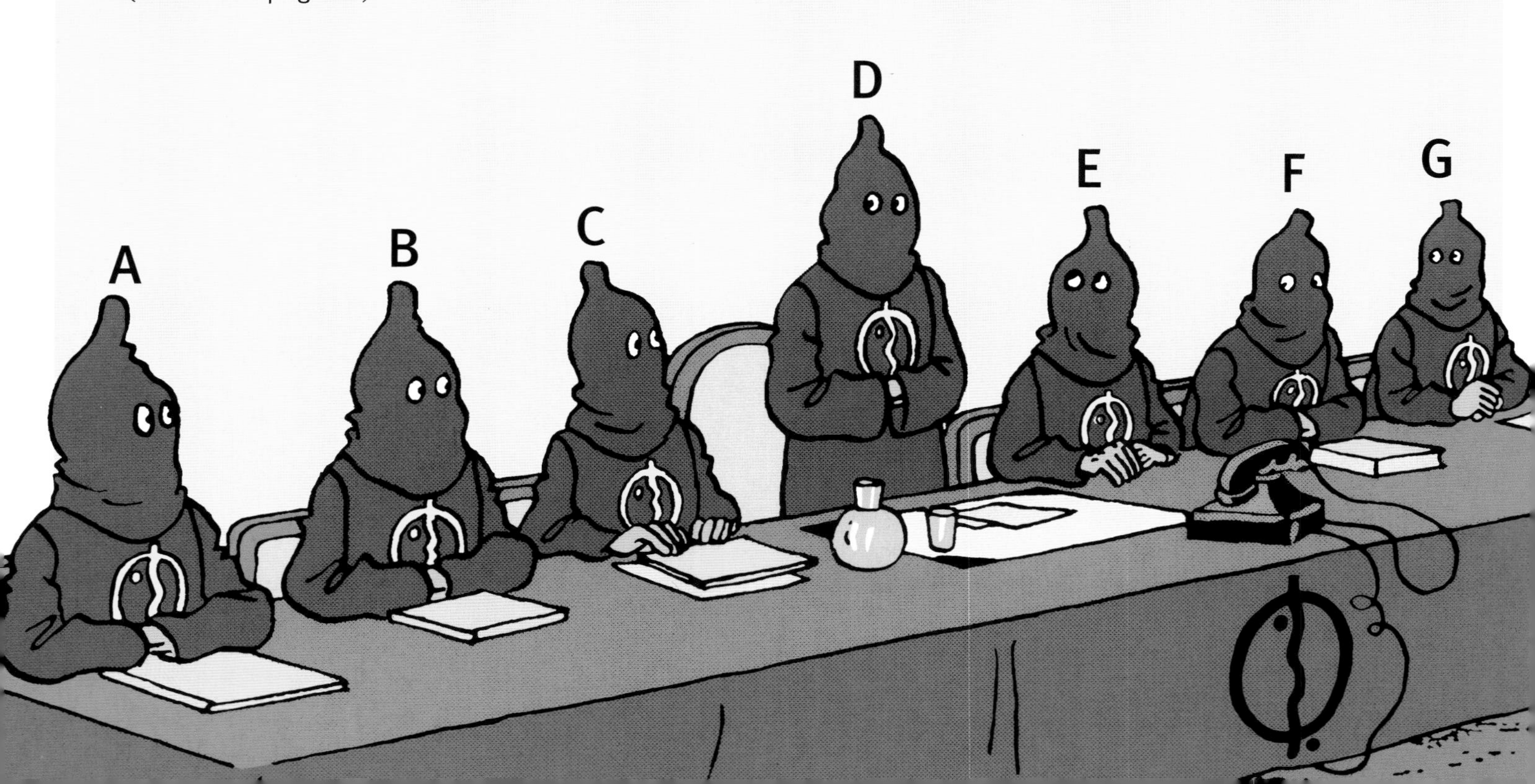

Fakir Word Search

The Fakir is trying to hypnotise Tintin and Snowy. Quick – solve the word search and release Tintin from the spell! (Answers on page 68)

C	S	C	A	I	R	O	E	T	B	U
M	I	L	S	N	O	W	Y	O	R	I
B	P	G	F	F	P	O	I	S	O	N
V	H	P	A	K	K	R	G	J	T	G
A	A	Y	T	R	L	M	C	Y	H	S
S	R	T	F	H	S	E	C	R	E	T
D	A	G	C	T	J	L	Y	G	R	T
P	O	I	K	I	H	O	S	K	H	U
R	H	E	U	N	P	K	E	B	O	R
S	O	F	E	T	S	H	S	R	O	L
D	F	A	K	I	R	L	E	J	D	L
I	M	L	U	N	F	D	A	R	T	R
P	M	A	D	N	E	S	S	N	M	C

TINTIN
SNOWY
FAKIR
BROTHERHOOD

POISON
CIGARS
CIPHER
CAIRO

MADNESS
SECRET
KIH-OSKH
PHARAOH

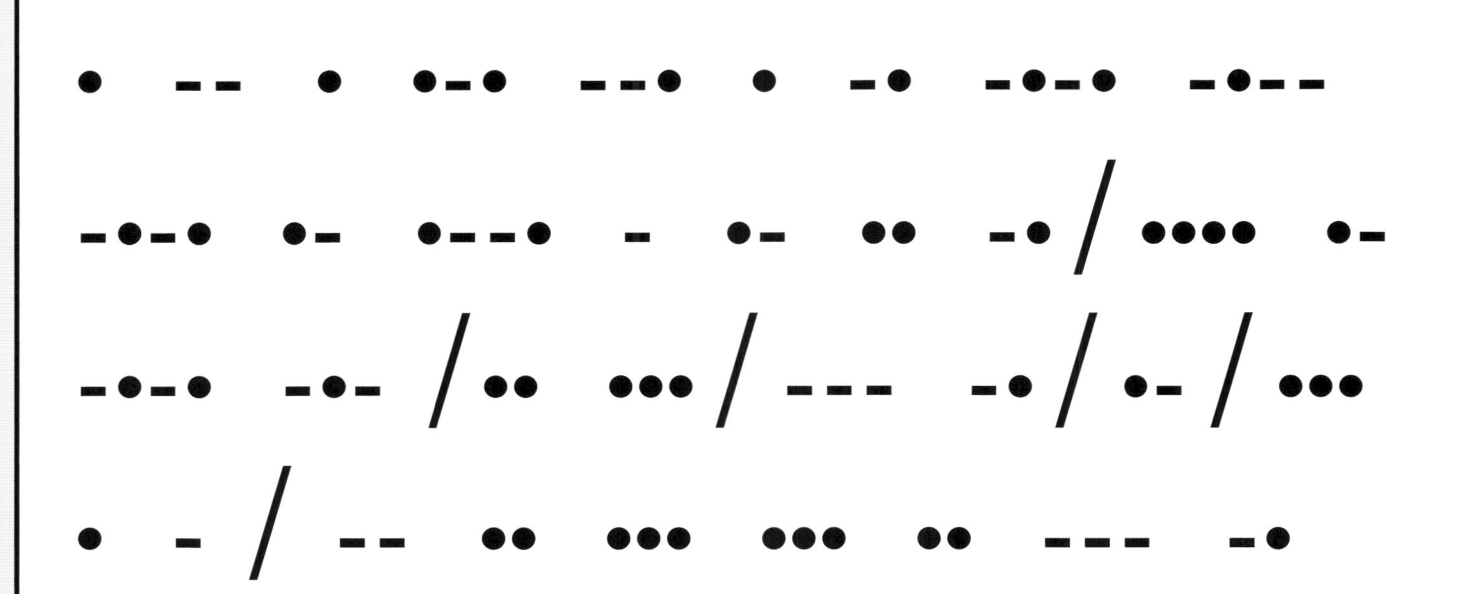

Tintin : Radio Officer

In *Land of Black Gold*, Tintin becomes the radio officer aboard the ship the *Speedol Star*. He uses a special transmitter to tap out messages in Morse code.

•–•–•–

–••   –••   –––

•   –•–•   •–•

Morse Mystery

Morse code is an international code for transmitting messages using short signals (dots) and long signals (dashes). Use the alphabet below to work out what the secret message says. You could also use it to write your own secret messages!

(See if you were right on page 68)

Morse code machine

History of the Code

The American artist and inventor Samuel Morse invented Morse code in 1835. Until 1999, ships all around the world used it as a simple way to communicate with each other.

A •–
B –•••
C –•–•
D –••
E •
F ••–•
G ––•
H ••••
I ••
J •–––
K –•–
L •–••
M ––
N –•
O –––
P •––•
Q ––•–
R •–•
S •••
T –
U ••–
V •••–
W •––
X –••–
Y –•––
Z ––••

0 ––––
1 •––––
2 ••–––
3 •••––
4 ••••–
5 •••••
6 –••••
7 ––•••
8 –––••
9 ––––•

Full stop •–•–•–

Land of the Pharaohs

In *Cigars of the Pharaoh*, Tintin travels to Egypt. He explores ancient tombs built more than 4,000 years ago, and discovers huge pyramids, mysterious mummies and statues of strange gods.

Egyptian Kings

In ancient times, Egypt was ruled by powerful kings and queens known as pharaohs. The pharaohs sometimes wore head-dresses decorated with cobra snakes and false beards.

Picture Writing

The Ancient Egyptians 'wrote' using a language made of pictures, known as hieroglyphics. Many of their temples and monuments were inscribed with this picture writing. After the Ancient Egyptians, people forgot how to read hieroglyphics. For hundreds of years, no one knew what they meant until a French scholar managed to crack the code in 1822.

The Secret of the Nile

Egypt is a desert country, so you would expect nothing to grow there. In fact, a mighty river called the Nile runs right through the desert.
Crops grow well along its banks, enabling people to live there since ancient times.
These people created a mighty civilisation known today as Ancient Egypt.

Tintin walks in the Egyptian desert near the giant pyramids.

Gods and Goddesses

The Ancient Egyptians worshipped thousands of gods and goddesses. They had a god for everything, and the gods were responsible for everything that happened. Here are just six of them:

Re
the falcon-headed sun god

Osiris
god of the Underworld, where the dead live

Isis
one of the great goddesses, wife of Osiris

Anubis
the jackal-headed god of the dead

Horus
god of the sky, in the form of a falcon

Bastet
a cat-goddess

Tintin & Snowy pass a large stone carving of an animal-headed god.

Here's one "mummy" that definitely was NOT made in ancient times!

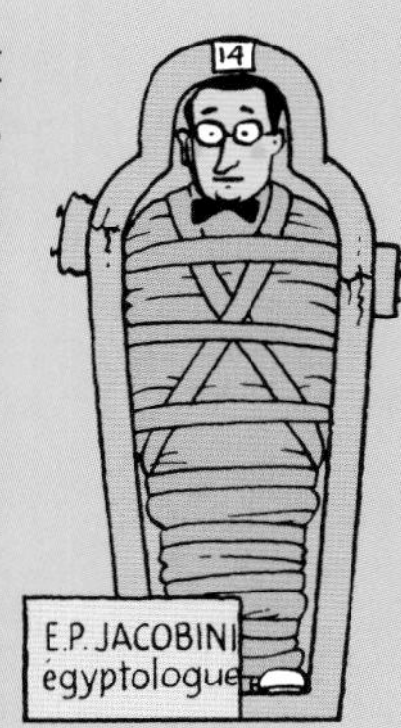

I Want My Mummy!

The Ancient Egyptians had a special way of looking after their dead. They wrapped them up very carefully in cloth.
This process is called mummification.
It preserved the body so that the person's spirit could live on.

The Pyramids

The Ancient Egyptian pharaohs were buried inside giant pyramid-shaped stone tombs. Since the king's gold and silver was also buried inside, the entrance was meant to be a secret. But thieves usually managed to sneak in!

Abdullah's Pranks

If there's one thing Abdullah knows, it's the best time to play a trick. And that is – all the time! With these great prank ideas, you can have lots of fun – at somebody else's expense! Just don't get caught...

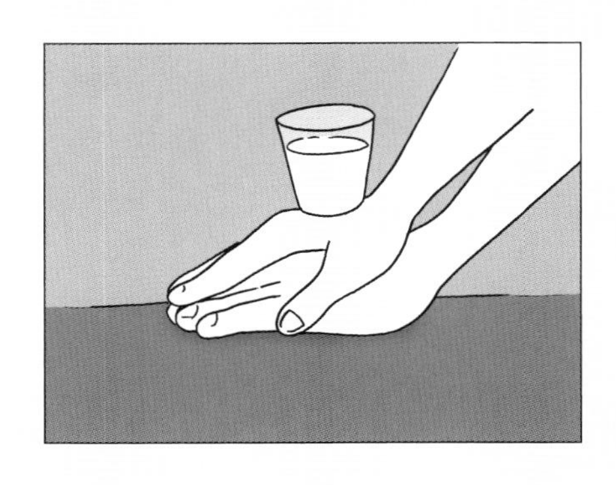

Water Trick

You will need:

- A plastic tumbler

Fill the tumbler with water. Then tell your victim you have a great trick to show them. Ask them to place one hand over the other, flat on top of a table – an outside table is best! Balance the tumbler on top of their hands. Then walk away. They will be stuck, and find it impossible to move without spilling the drink!

Fat Head

You will need:
- thin strips of old newspaper
- sticky tape

A simple but effective trick, guaranteed to fool anyone who wears a hat or cap. Stick the paper strips inside the hat and watch the wearer wonder why their hat has shrunk!

Early Alarm

You will need:
- all the clocks in the house!

Here's a good one for April Fool's Day. Get up early and reset all the clocks in the house to one hour earlier. Watch the confusion!

Exploding Cushion

You will need:
- a paper bag
- sticky tape
- crunchy breakfast cereal

This is an easy-to-prepare trick. All you need is a paper bag and some breakfast cereal. Fill the bag with the cereal; seal it shut with sticky tape, and place it under a cushion on a chair. Then just wait until someone sits down... CRUUU-NNN-CCHHH!

A tip from Abdullah – choose who you decide to play a trick on carefully. Make sure they cannot run as fast as you!

Seeing Spots

Ayesha is a tame cheetah. But you must never steal her dinner – which is just what Snowy does. Then Ayesha is not so tame! Follow the ropes to find out which one is attached to Ayesha.

(Answer on page 68)

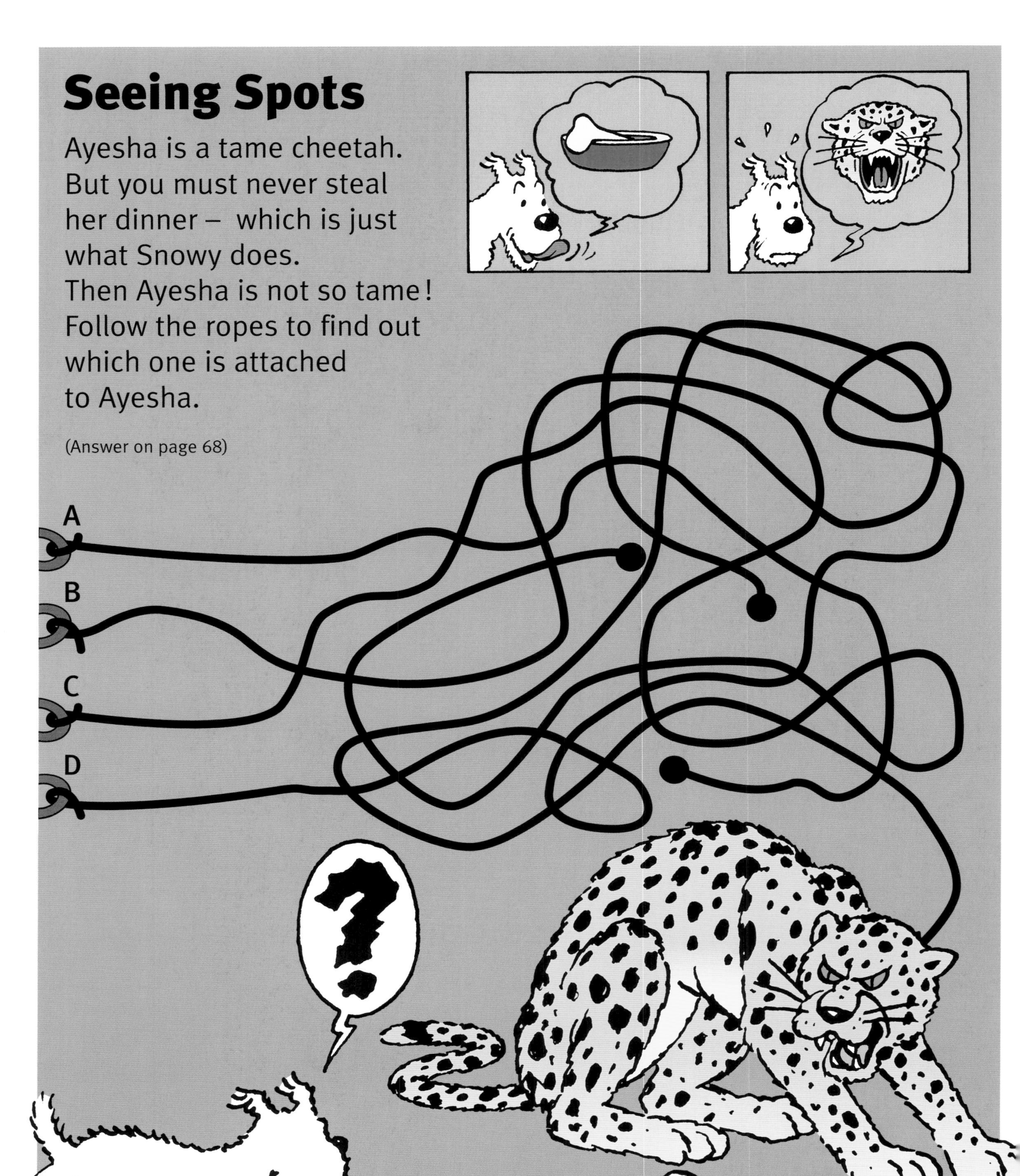

Mirror Muddle

One fine morning, Captain Haddock is cleaning his teeth when – CRASH! What's happened to the bathroom mirror? And what's happened to the story panels? They're out of order. Can you put them in the right order?

1

(Answer on page 68)

2

3

4

5

6

7

8

9

Explorers on the Moon

TINTIN IS GOING to the Moon. The great day has come. In a few hours the boy reporter and his friends will board the rocket designed by Professor Cuthbert Calculus, inventor and scientist. The huge rocket stands ready on the launch pad, pointing towards the stars. The world waits as the little band of moon explorers – Tintin, Snowy, Captain Haddock and Professor Calculus – prepare for their hazardous journey. Mr Baxter, head of Mission Control, proposes a toast, "Good luck to our Moon-Rocket – and a safe return!"

Aboard the spacecraft, which is about to blast off, Tintin whispers to Snowy, "Between you and me, I'm scared stiff!" And there's certainly plenty to worry about. What if the Professor has made a terrible mistake in his calculations? Will the rocket explode on take-off? Suppose, as Captain Haddock gloomily predicts, they all go wandering off between the Great Bear and the Milky Way and never return to Earth . . .

Meanwhile, the rocket is ready to go. The area is cleared. The countdown proceeds . . . Five minutes to lift-off . . . All systems checked . . . The world holds its breath . . . Lying flat on their bunks the astronauts listen tensely to the beating of their own hearts . . . One minute to go . . . Eight seconds . . . seven . . . six . . . five . . . four . . . three . . . two . . . one . . . ZERO! Ignition! Lift-off!

Slowly, majestically, the great rocket rises . . . then gathers speed, faster and faster, streaking into the darkness, propelled by the fantastic power of its jets. Soon the Professor's great invention, the nuclear motor, will take over. Already the sight of the distant Earth is incredibly beautiful. But nobody in the rocket is watching the view. They are not watching anything at all. Blacked-out by the crushing force of acceleration on lift-off, the crew lies unconscious in the cabin. Guided only by computers, the rocket hurtles into the vastness of space. No one moves . . . No one? That's not quite true. Someone aboard the rocket is awake, someone who hasn't completely blacked-out. Snowy! Mission Control call the Moon-Rocket, but Snowy has no time for them. His first thought is for Tintin, who is unconscious on his bunk. The radio calls become more and more urgent: "Earth calling Moon-Rocket . . . Are you receiving me? Come in please . . ." But the rocket is silent and the space travellers show no signs of life.

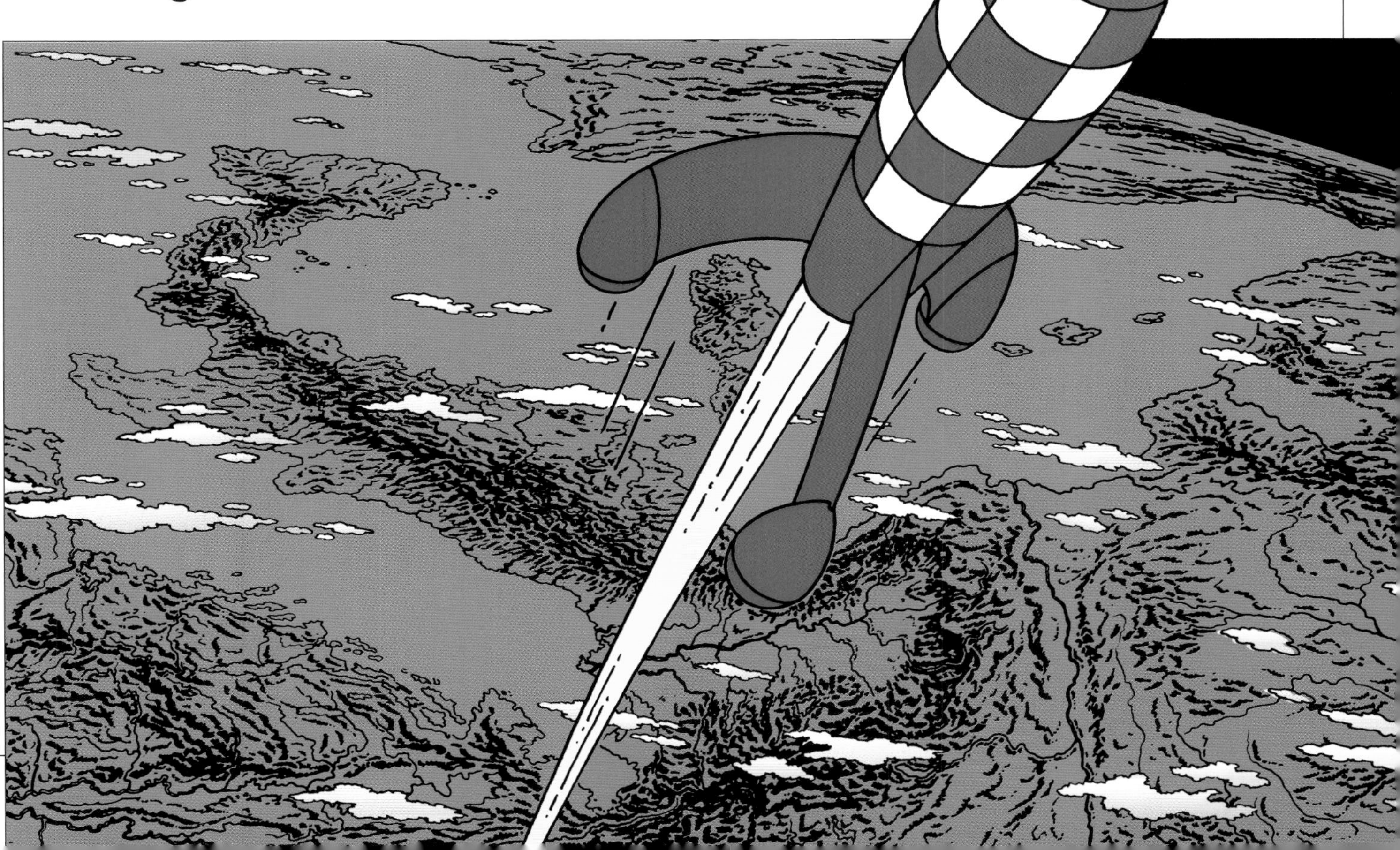

The radio calls begin once more: "Earth calling Moon-Rocket . . . Are you receiving me? Come in, please . . . Come in, please." Suddenly, a reply. But not the one they are expecting, "Woah! Woah! Woah!"

It's Snowy, barking in his master's ear, frantically trying to rouse him. He climbs on to Tintin's back and licks his face, "Tintin! Tintin! Wake up! You must wake up!" And then, success – Tintin opens his eyes.

The rocket is now 3,000 miles from the Earth. The crew have all recovered. Mission Control confirms, "Your position is exactly as estimated – you are on course for the Moon."

Not a single hitch: the Professor is delighted. But not for long – here comes trouble! A trap-door lifts, and before the astonished crew two familiar figures clamber into view: Thomson and Thompson, the detectives. They were having a quiet snoop round the rocket on the ground, but forgot to check what time it was leaving. They pose a serious problem. Will there be enough oxygen with two extra passengers? Captain Haddock is purple with fury.

"You brace of brontosauruses, you!" he roars. "Blistering barnacles! When I think that I'm forbidden to smoke one tiny little pipe, on the pretext of saving oxygen – the very same oxygen you two come here and gulp down!"

Professor Calculus is up in the control cabin. "Here, quickly," he calls. "Come and see this. Have a look in the stroboscopic periscope." They gather round to see an incredible sight.

Six thousand miles away the Earth shines like a blue jewel. They see the asteroid Adonis and the Moon, their distant target. The sky is filled with millions of stars, and a meteor streaks across the heavens.

But something's wrong! Those clumsy detectives have meddled with the controls and stopped the nuclear motor. The artificial gravity in the rocket is cut off.

Everything floats about in a state of weightlessness, with the crew doing an unexpected flying ballet.

And now more trouble... Whisky! Smoking and drinking are strictly forbidden on the rocket. But the Captain couldn't resist the temptation to smuggle a bottle or two aboard. And now he's had one drink too many, with horrifying results. Tintin finds a note: "I'm fed up with your rotten rocket. I'm going home to Marlinspike!" Signed: Haddock.

Sure enough he's gone! Without a moment's hesitation, Tintin puts on his spacesuit and climbs out of the rocket. There is the Captain, walking back to Earth!

Tintin contacts the Professor by radio, "I can see the Captain. He's floating along about thirty feet from the rocket, going at the same speed as us. I'll do all I can to get him back . . ."

However, they haven't reckoned with Adonis, the asteroid they saw in the periscope. A rocky mass about two thousand feet in diameter, Adonis is a fragment torn from an ancient planet that orbited long ago between Mars and Jupiter.

Professor Calculus spots it first, "Goodness gracious, there's Adonis!"

"Who's he?" asks Thompson.
"One of your friends who lives round here?"

But the asteroid is a deadly enemy. Its gravitational pull draws the Captain further and further from the rocket. "Naturally," comments Calculus, "he's going into orbit round the asteroid. I must tell Earth that Adonis has a new satellite named 'Haddock'."

"No," calls Tintin. "Raise the retractable ladder so I can anchor myself. Then start the motor, increase speed gently until I can get close enough to the Captain to throw a line and pull him aboard."
The Professor obeys reluctantly, "It's sheer madness, you know, but you can try . . ."

The hazardous operation is carried out. Tintin lassoes the Captain and hauls him, protesting furiously, back to the rocket!

As the rocket nears its goal, Professor Calculus begins the delicate manoeuvres for touchdown. With the spacecraft on course for the middle of a large crater, auxiliary jets fire to break the descent. Again the crew black out, but controlled by the automatic pilot, the rocket makes a perfect three-point landing on the surface of the Moon.

The crew soon recover and radio communication is re-established. Professor Calculus talks to Mr Baxter at Mission Control,
"Now we are going to disembark from the rocket. The honour has fallen to the youngest among us: we have chosen Tintin to be the first to set foot on the Moon."

Tintin and Snowy put on their spacesuits and enter the airlock. The air pressure is reduced to zero and the outside door swings slowly on its hinges.

"What a fantastic sight!" Tintin describes the scene, "It's a nightmare land, a place of death, horrifying in its desolation . . . Not a tree, not a flower, not a blade of grass . . . No sound at all . . ."

The retractable ladder slides into position and Tintin slowly climbs down. Three rungs to go . . . two rungs . . . one rung . . . Now!

"This is it!" shouts Tintin. "For the first time in the history of mankind, there is an EXPLORER ON THE MOON!"

(Continued on page 48)

condor

Bird Brains

Whether they're winged warriors or feathered friends, airborne animals make many appearances in Tintin's adventures. But how keen a birdwatcher are you? Find out with this quack – er, quick picture quiz?

1 Although I am a bird, I cannot fly.

2 My young are known as cygnets.

CHAK-CHAK

magpie

penguin

How to Play

Read the statements and try to guess which animal is saying each one. You'll learn some fun facts to impress your friends!

Don't get into a flap if you're not sure. Fly on over to page 68 for the answers.

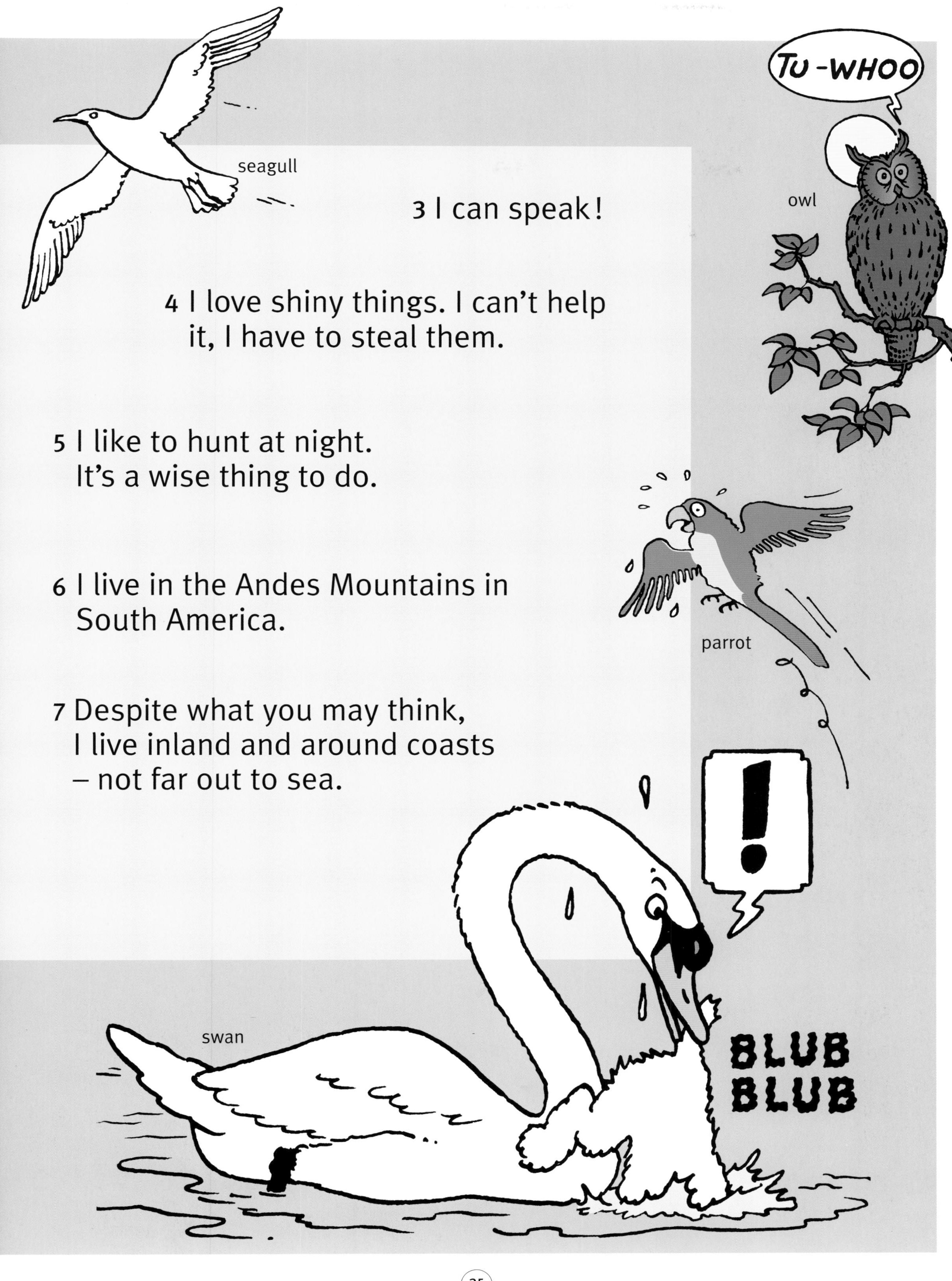

3 I can speak!

4 I love shiny things. I can't help it, I have to steal them.

5 I like to hunt at night. It's a wise thing to do.

6 I live in the Andes Mountains in South America.

7 Despite what you may think, I live inland and around coasts – not far out to sea.

Light Fantastic!

Scientists like Cuthbert Calculus have studied light for centuries. Here are two fun projects that will teach you about light and shadows. (A shadow is a patch of darkness, which is formed when something gets in the way of light.)

Spider Shadow Shape

This spider shape casts a spooky shadow on the wall. Make the shadow bigger or smaller by moving the torch.

You will need:

- black card
- a pencil
- black cotton thread or string
- sticky tape
- a torch
- scissors

1 Use a pencil to draw the outline of a spider on a piece of black card. Make the spider as large as you can!

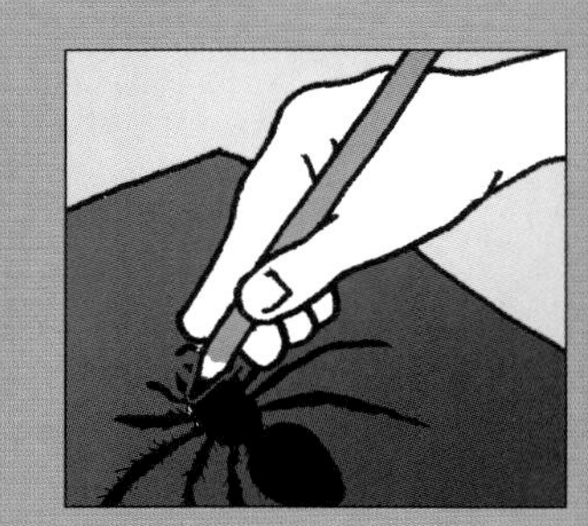

2 Ask an adult to carefully cut around the outline with a pair of scissors.

3 Use sticky tape to attach a piece of black cotton or string to the spider shape.

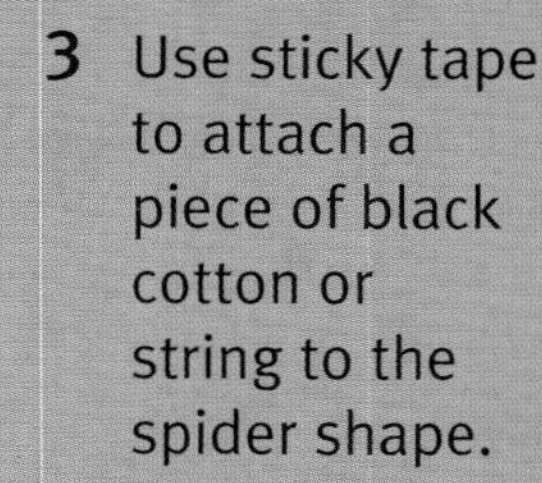

4 Hang or dangle your spider in front of a torch in a dark room with white walls. Look for the spooky shadow!

Tintin jumps at the sight of a gigantic spider!

Make a Sundial

Since ancient times, people have used sundials to tell the time. Sundials work by using a pointer to cast a shadow from the sun. As the sun moves across the sky, the shadow moves round the dial like the hand of a clock.

You will need:

- two pieces of thick card
- pair of compasses
- pencil and pen
- scissors
- strong glue
- compass
- ruler
- paints and paintbrush

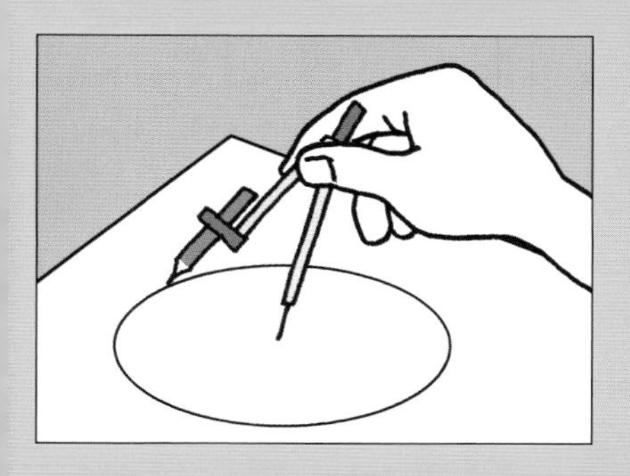

1 Set a pair of compasses to 10cm and use them to draw a circle on a piece of card. Carefully cut out the circle with scissors.

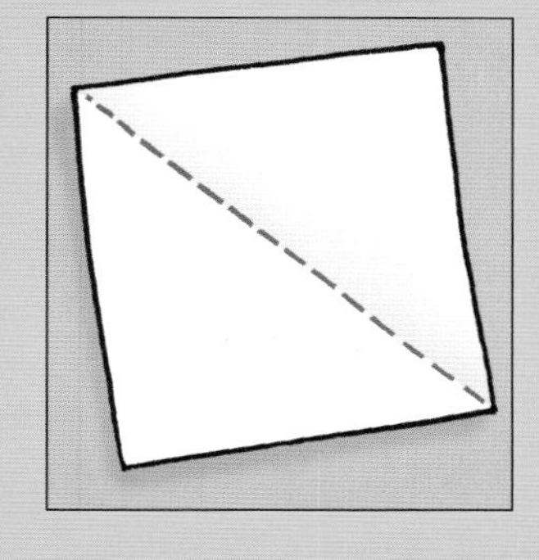

2 Draw a 10cm x 10cm square on the card. Draw a diagonal line across it to make two triangles.

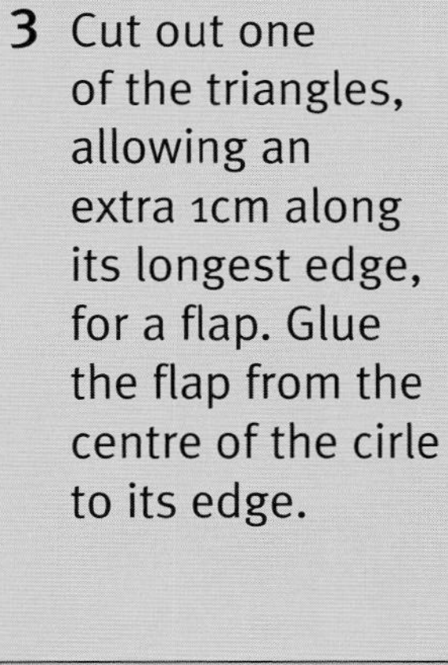

3 Cut out one of the triangles, allowing an extra 1cm along its longest edge, for a flap. Glue the flap from the centre of the cirle to its edge.

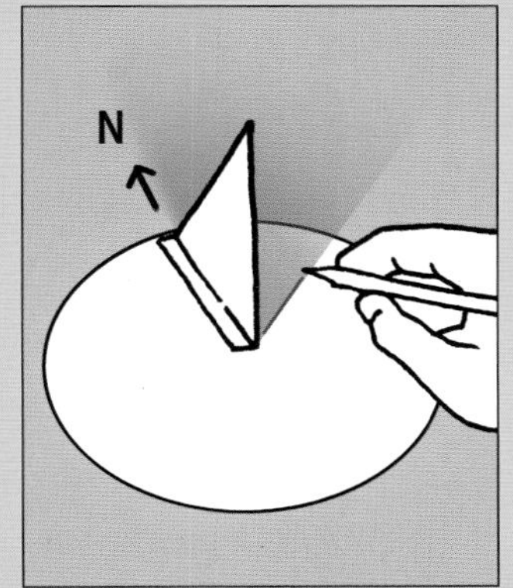

4 Use a compass to turn the sundial so the pointer points North. Draw a straight line at the edge of the shadow.

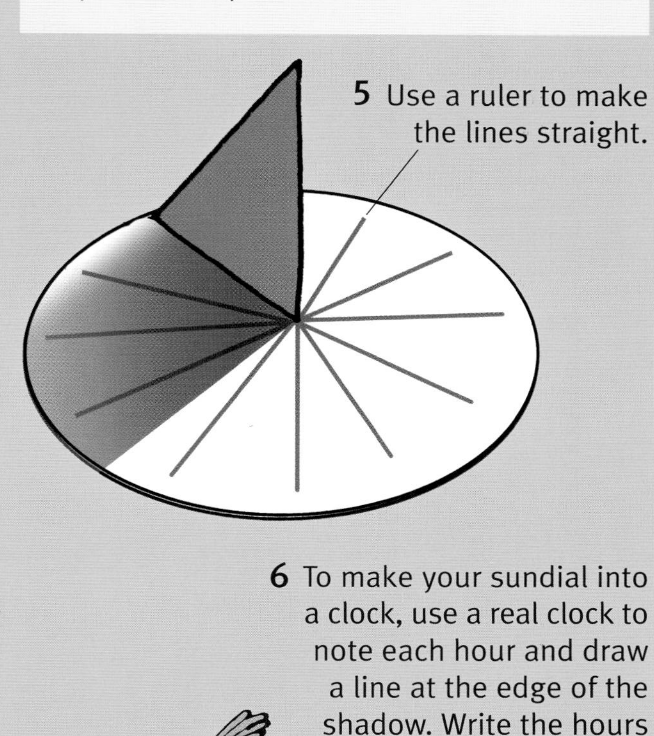

5 Use a ruler to make the lines straight.

6 To make your sundial into a clock, use a real clock to note each hour and draw a line at the edge of the shadow. Write the hours by each line. You could decorate your sundial with paints!

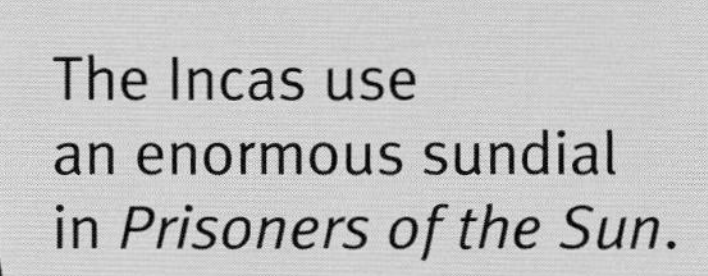

The Incas use an enormous sundial in *Prisoners of the Sun*.

Daring Escape!

Help Tintin escape from the mob – on the OUTSIDE of the building. Starting at A, find the path through the gaps in the bricks to take you to B.

(Answer on page 68)

A
B

Exploring the Moon

In *Explorers on the Moon*, Tintin and Haddock travel to the Moon in a rocket. The Moon is a cold, dry globe whose surface is pock-marked with craters and strewn with rocks and dust.
The Moon orbits the Earth at a distance of 384,400 km. Want to know more? Then read on!

One side of the moon is always facing the Earth.

Craters

The Moon's surface is covered with millions of dents, called craters. Craters are caused when space rocks crash into the Moon. The largest crater is more than 2,000 km wide.

The Moon has no wind so Tintin's footprints will never blow away.

Moon Walk

Thomson and Thompson can leap and jump like superheroes on the Moon. This is because gravity – the force that keeps us firmly on the ground on Earth – is six times weaker on the Moon.

Underground Ice

Tintin and Snowy discover underground ice caverns on the Moon. Even though the Moon looks as dry as a desert, some scientists think water or ice might lie beneath its surface. The water could have come from meteorites.

Staring Into Space

Calculus uses a telescope to look deep into space. It would be much easier to look into space from a telescope on the Moon. Telescopes on Earth must look through the thick gases that make up the atmosphere, but the Moon has no atmosphere to block the view!

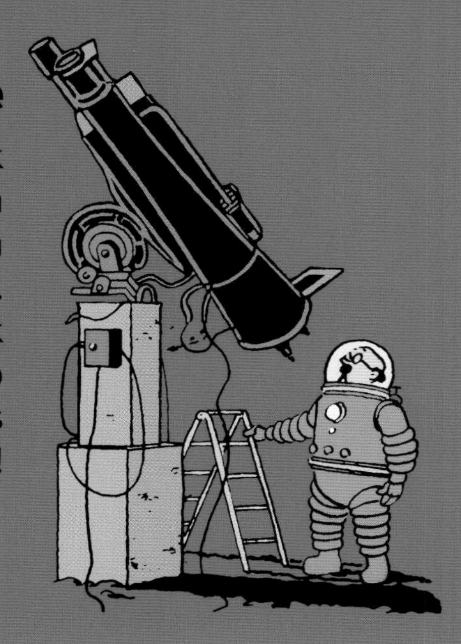

More Moon Facts

- The Moon is the second brightest object in the sky after the Sun, but the Moon does not produce its own light. It only looks bright because it reflects light from the Sun.
- Temperatures are more extreme on the Moon than on Earth. They range from -173° Celsius at night to more than 100° Celsius (above the boiling point of water!).
- It takes about two days to fly to the Moon in a rocket. If you could drive there by car, it would take 135 days!

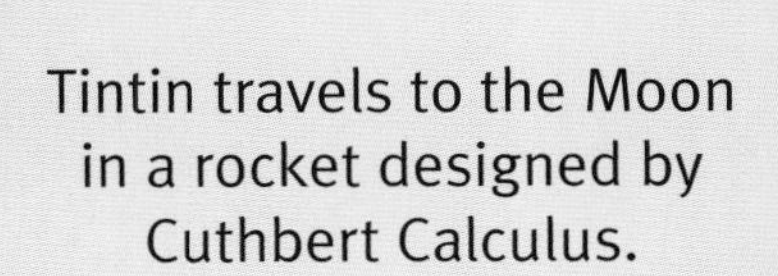

Tintin travels to the Moon in a rocket designed by Cuthbert Calculus.

Memorable Journey

When Tintin and Haddock are picked up by a driver in a strange country, Tintin memorises each turn the car takes so he knows the way back – in case of trouble.

Can you work out where Tintin and Haddock end up by following Tintin's notes:

"Hmm, first a left turn. Slight bend in the road, then a right turn. Look, another right turn. Now a right turn. Left at the junction (I'm sure I've seen this road before!). Now first left. Left at the fork. Along a bendy road. Straight over…"

(Answer on page 68)

BH 15
F
E
D
C
ЮЕРХВЕН
ВЕРТЗРАГЗ
SLOW
ROAD WORKS
ФОРВОТЗЕН
ЗОНА
SECURITY
AREA

1

2

5

6

Up-close and Personal

Here's a line-up of familiar characters from Tintin's adventures. But can you work out who the enlarged sections belongs to?

When you think you've worked, it out, turn to page 68 to see if you were right.

Cuthbert Calculus Tintin Snowy

3
4
7
8
Nestor
Thompson
Thomson
Bianca Castafiore
Captain Haddock

Stop Tintin !

A gang of crooks wants Tintin out of the way. So begins a fiendish game of cat and mouse. Play this equally fiendish board game – you can either be Tintin or the villains!

How to Play

Choose your counters below.
One player moves Tintin, the other moves the three villains.

Tintin starts on the white circle;
the villains start on the yellow circles.
Players take it in turns to move.
Tintin can move 2 spaces in any direction.
The villains may make 3 moves at each turn: either one villain can move 3 spaces, two villains can move 1 space and 2 spaces each, or three villains can move 1 space each etc.

The villains win if they trap Tintin so he cannot move. Tintin wins if he reaches the blue circle without being surrounded by the villains.

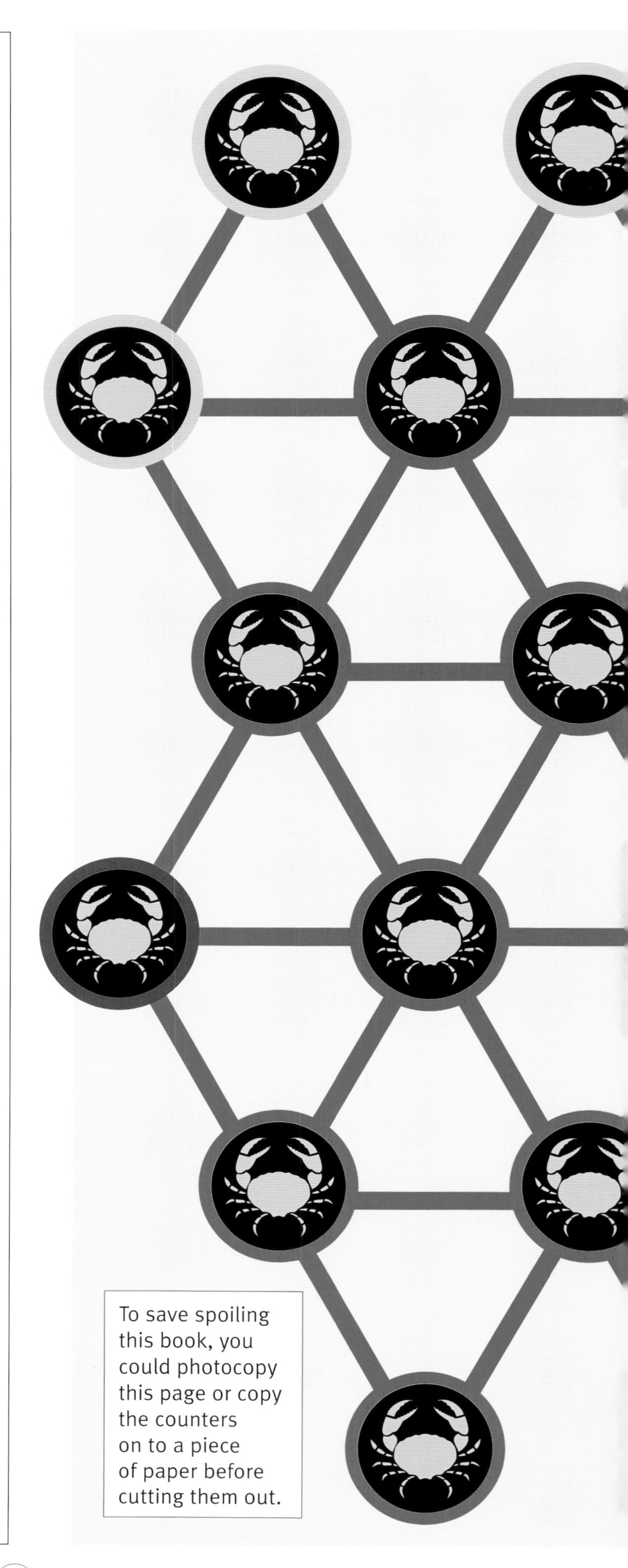

To save spoiling this book, you could photocopy this page or copy the counters on to a piece of paper before cutting them out.

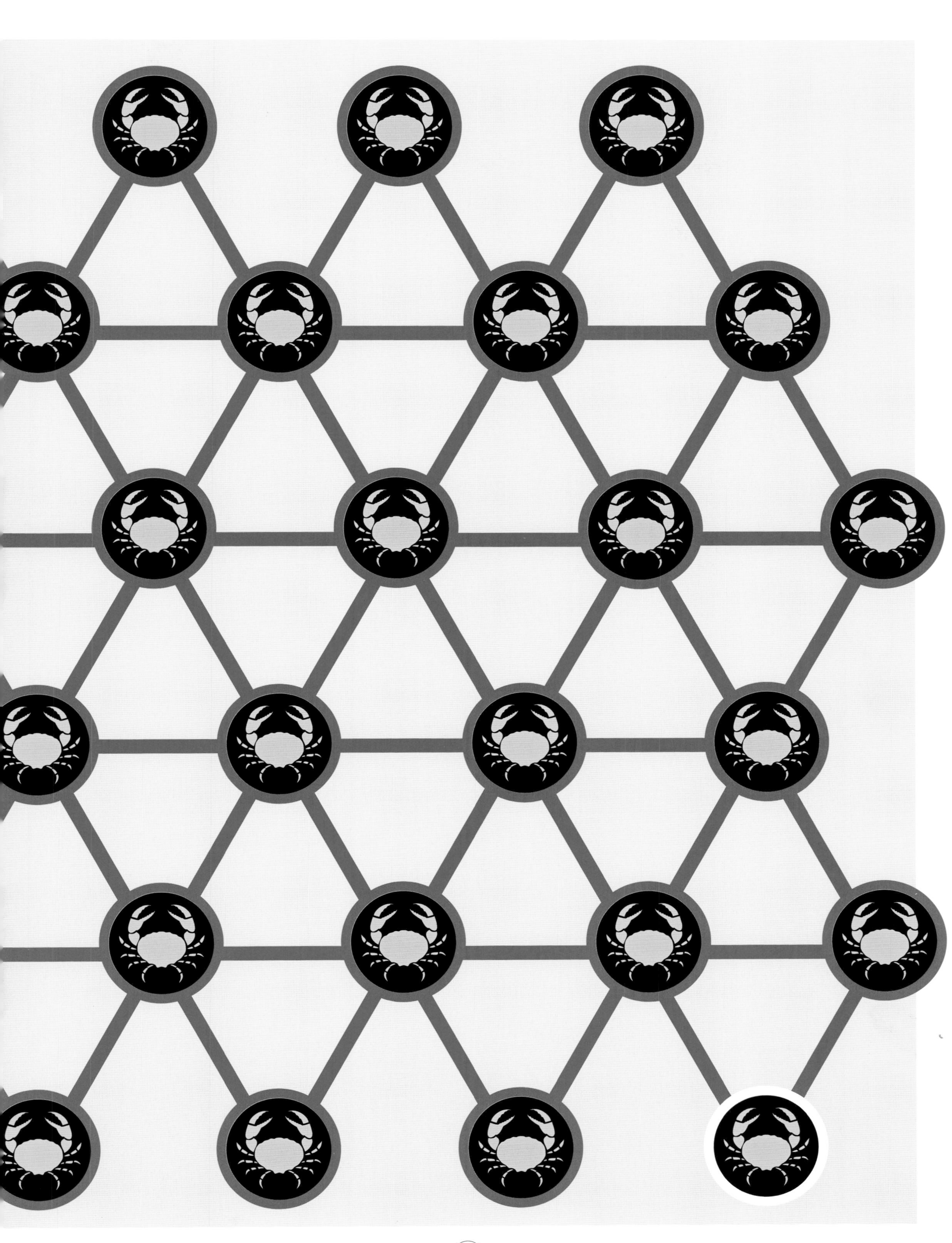

Explorers on the Moon

(Continued from page 32)

THE EXPLORERS DISEMBARK. Thomson and Thompson soon discover one of the Moon's surprises: with gravity only a sixth of that on Earth, when they start to walk they jump like kangaroos!

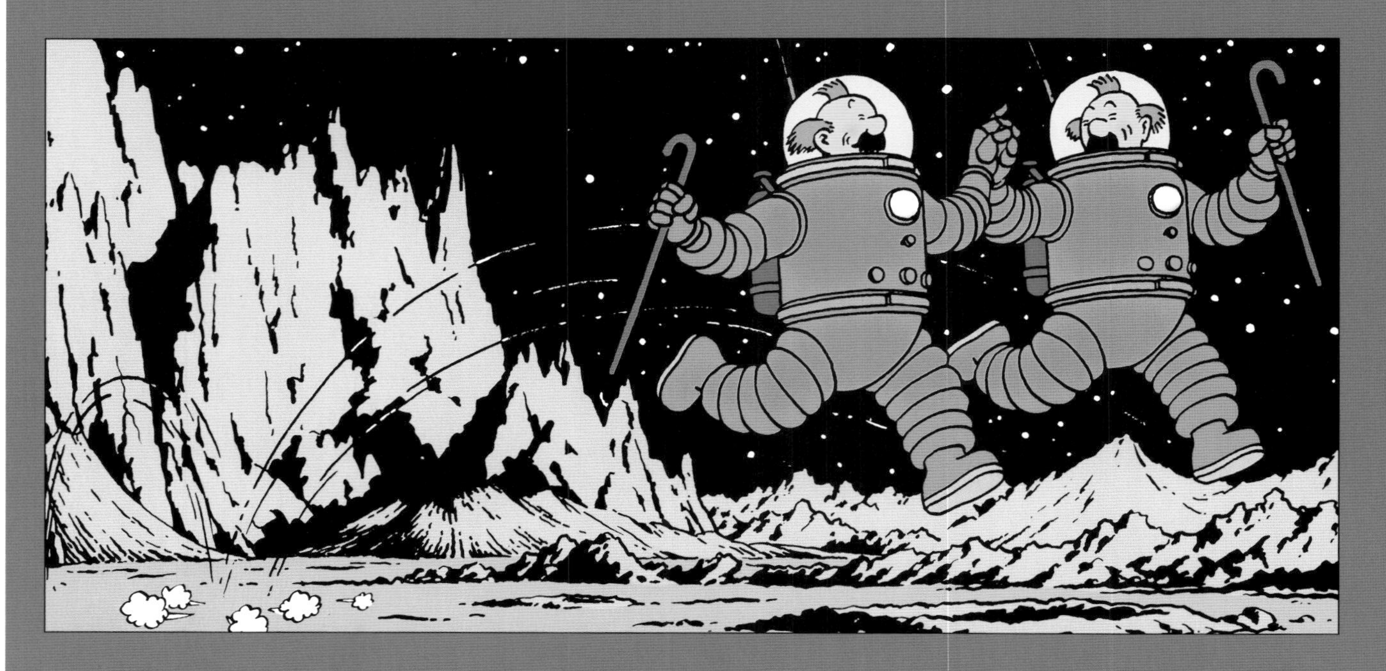

But, to work! Tintin and his friends haven't much time, less than one day in fact. But that is a lunar day, equal to fourteen on Earth. Even so, they must hurry before their oxygen runs out. Supplies were calculated for the regular crew, without two accidental stowaways!

Equipment is unloaded: scientific apparatus first, with the sections of the special reconnaissance vehicle. Professor Calculus is soon busy setting up the telescope for the lunar observatory. He reports to Earth, "The reconnaissance tank is ready. We're going to make the first trials. Tintin has just entered the turret. He will be in command and take the controls. The Captain will act as lookout."

The hatch on the tank is secured and the pressurised cabin filled with air. Now it is safe for the explorers to remove their spacesuits.

The Professor continues, “I can see the Captain’s head through the multiplex cockpit, over. He’s smiling and signalling that everything’s in order. Now we’re really going to explore the Moon!”

Tintin steers the tank over the bumpy lunar surface. “Billions of blistering blue barnacles!” snorts Captain Haddock, as he bumps his head. “Can’t you drive more smoothly?”

On a brief expedition from the tank, the Captain follows Tintin into a vast cave filled with stalagmites and stalactites. “Look!” says Tintin. “There must once have been water on the Moon.”

Snowy goes to explore on his own. Tintin calls him back, “Be careful, stay close to us.” Snowy isn’t pleased. “Honestly! What does he take me for? Granny’s little lap-dog?”

Suddenly, a crevasse opens beneath Snowy’s feet and he disappears! Tintin and the Captain dash to the rescue. Tintin climbs down into the crevasse and to his astonishment lands on a sheet of ice. He falls flat on his back and slides to the bottom, feet in the air, to join the missing Snowy. The Captain’s comments, as he hauls them out, are enough to melt the ice!

Time goes by . . . and the lunar night begins to fall on the desolate moonscape. Final readings are taken before the equipment is dismantled. The tank is to be abandoned on the Moon, so Tintin leaves a message in it, a record of the expedition’s adventures for other explorers who may follow.

The moment for departure draws near. The crew members take up their stations in the rocket. Lying flat on his bunk once more, Professor Calculus prepares to activate the jets for lift-off, listening intently to the countdown transmitted by radio operators at Mission Control back on Earth. “Five seconds to go . . . four . . . three . . . two . . . one . . . ZERO! Ignition! Lift-off!”

“Into the hands of fate!” says Professor Calculus. “I press this button, and pray that everything works. Otherwise we’re condemned to death!”

At Mission Control, the situation looks bleak. While the explorers lie unconscious after lift-off, the rocket veers off course. Was the steering gear damaged on landing? Maybe the gyroscopes aren’t working . . .

White-faced, Mr Baxter turns to the technicians, “The rocket is getting further and further away! Poor devils, they will be lost in space!”

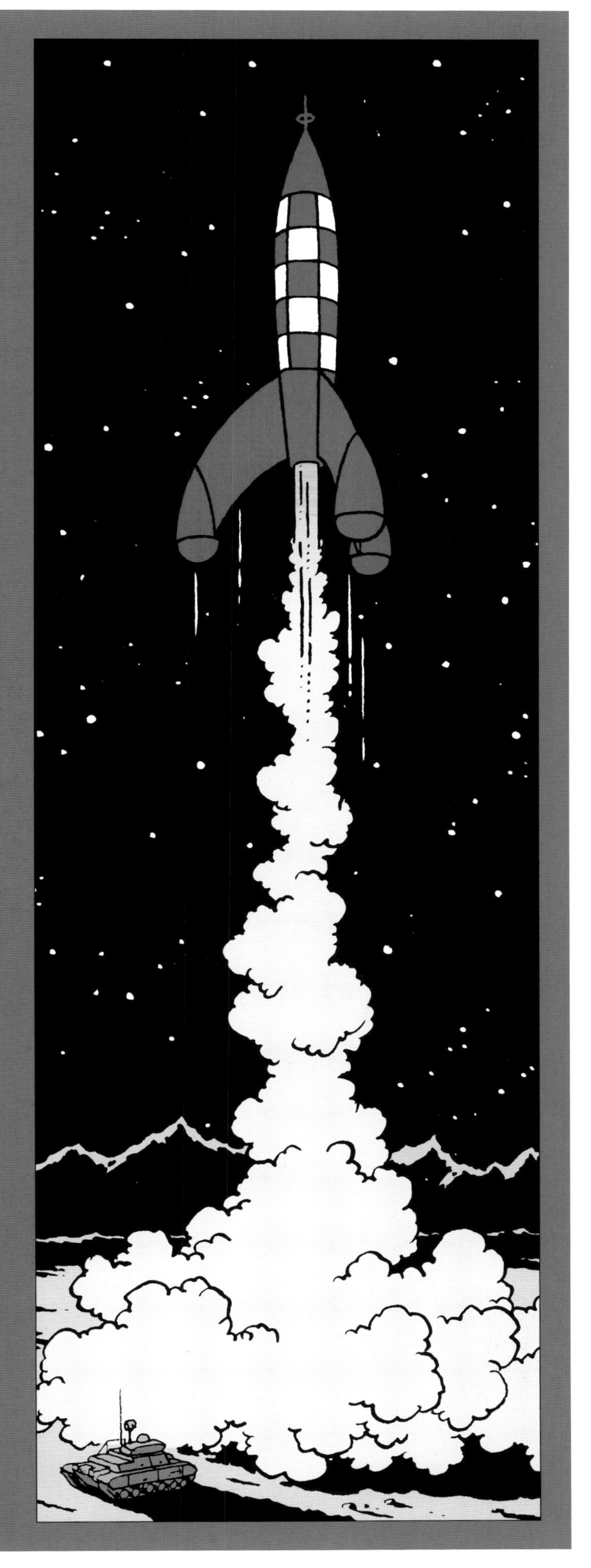

Suddenly Tintin answers the ceaseless radio calls, “Quickly,” Mr Baxter urges, “correct your line of flight. You are hopelessly off course!”

Tintin rouses the Professor, who makes a swift calculation. The rocket is on its way to Jupiter! He adjusts the controls and the Professor reports, “Moon-Rocket to Earth. The steering was jammed. We are now heading for home!”

The long journey passes uneventfully. As the rocket shoots towards Earth, Mission Control encourages the crew, “Keep your spirits up! Only two hours and you will be back!”

Nearly home . . . but nearly out of oxygen! Gasping for breath, Tintin makes one final effort and reaches the control cabin to set the automatic pilot.
All eyes are on the sky . . . waiting . . . waiting. Seconds drag like hours. Suddenly, it’s there! Mr Baxter leaps into his car and races to the landing site. Amid billowing smoke and with an ear-shattering roar, the spacecraft touches down. Calculus’s rocket has proved itself. The Professor’s spacecraft has carried its crew to the Moon and back.

But what about the explorers? No one replies to the urgent radio calls from Mission Control. Have they all perished at the moment of victory? Mr Baxter climbs rapidly up the ladder. He lifts the hatch . . .

In the cabin, the crew all lie like corpses. Tintin's body is near the controls. Mr Baxter doesn't hesitate. "Oxygen! Get them out of here – they need oxygen!" Soon, they are all restored to life, except for the Captain. It takes whisky to bring him round!

Mission completed, so now it's time to celebrate. Professor Calculus makes a speech, "Here's to us all, explorers on the Moon! The marks of our feet are inscribed on the surface of our satellite. And I promise you, one day we shall return!"

The Captain nearly goes berserk, "WHAT? Go back? Us? To the Moon? Blistering barnacles – you and your interplanetary perambulator. I've had enough! I've learned just one thing from all this: our proper place is on dear old Earth. And that's where I'm staying! No more adventures for me!"

Tintin isn't so sure. "I wonder, Captain – haven't we heard that somewhere before?"

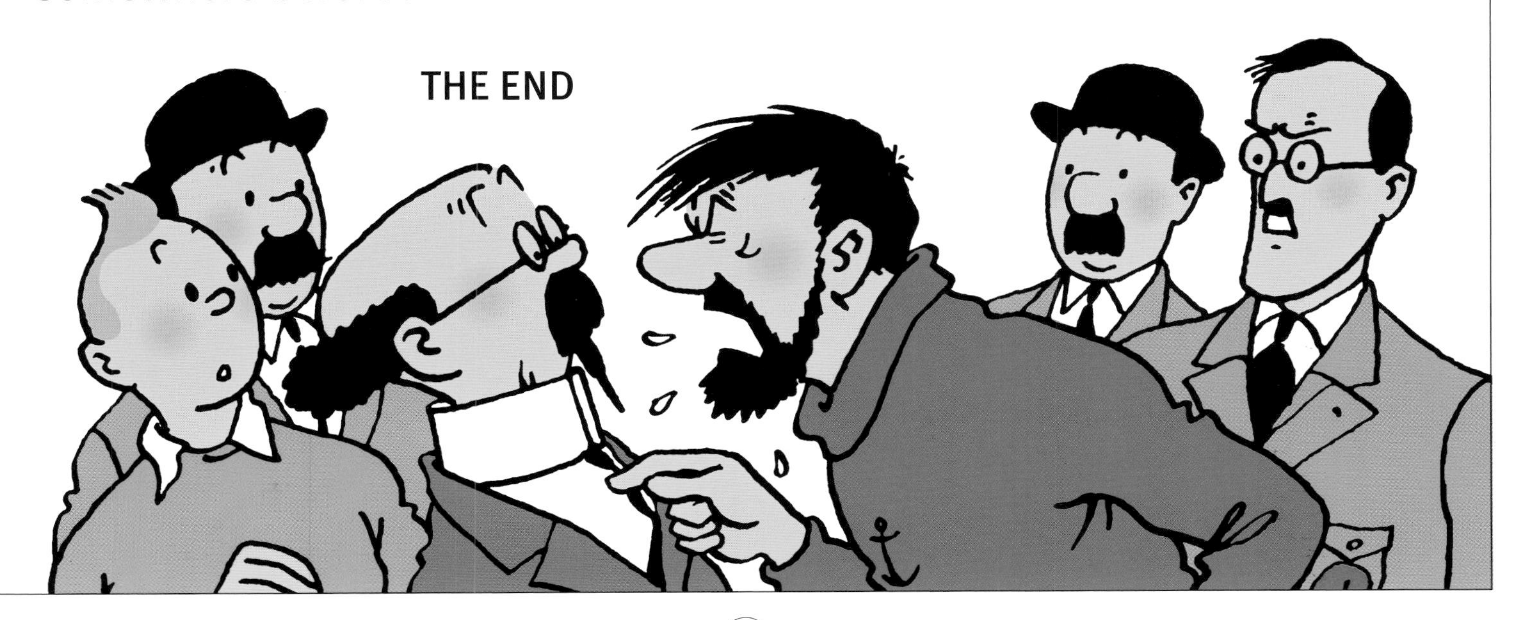

Ship-shape

When Tintin and Captain Haddock set off in search of Red Rackham's treasure, they hire a fishing boat called a trawler. These steam-powered boats carry large nets, which are floated on the sea behind it.

Steering

Tintin is at the wheel, steering the ship. Handles around the edge of the wheel allow a firm grip, even in strong winds.

Telegraph cables for sending and receiving messages

Funnel

Mizzen (second) mast

Hoist

Fishing boats use cranes to lower their nets into the water. Tintin and the crew are using their crane to lift the shark submarine into the sea.

Lifeboats

Steam trawlers always carry lifeboats – though they are not usually used for sleeping in!

Look Out!

The wheelhouse, where the steering wheel is found, looks out to the front of the ship.

Ship Funnel

Steamships are powered by coal. Big engines lie below deck. Boiler smoke or engine exhaust comes out through a funnel. The funnel can be seen in the middle of the picture.

Living Quarters

Calculus sits in his cabin, in front of his window, called a porthole. Windows on ships are made of thick glass so that they withstand storms.

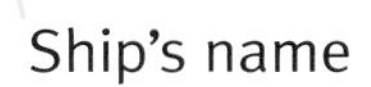

Direction-finding

Haddock uses a special measuring device called a sextant to work out the ship's position.

Winch

Calculus and Haddock stand in front of the winch, which pulls in the fishing nets when they are full.

Double Vision

Use the grid to help you draw Thomson and Thompson. They look identical, but are they? Hint : look carefully at the moustaches. If you photocopy the grid, you can make your drawing larger or smaller.

Pardon ?

As we all know, Professor Cuthbert Calculus is not deaf . . . just “a little hard of hearing in one ear”. So it’s all the more notable when he does, very occasionally, mishear something. Here’s a short puzzle – it has to be short, because, of course, it’s *so hard* to find examples of the Professor’s aural muddles. (No, not puddles . . . muddles . . . MUDDLES ! Oh never mind !)

Each question begins with a quote from Calculus – it’s what he thinks he’s heard. Then there are three possibilities for what was really said or done (A, B or C). Can you guess which one it is ?

(Answers on page 68)

SCORE (out of 7) :

0 **Terrible.** You’re just acting the goat !

1–2 **Must try harder.** There, heard that didn’t you ?

3–4 **Promising.** But you might still need an ear trumpet.

5–6 **Well done.** You seem to have an ear for it.

7 **Congratulations !** You’ve graduated with top marks, Professor !

1 “Hello, there’s a storm brewing.”

A A telephone rings
B Snowy growls
C Captain Haddock sings the Jewel Song from Faust

2 “Gone away ?”

A Tintin says “good day!”
B Haddock asks Calculus his name
C Tintin warns Calculus to get out of the way

3 “A bath? That’s a good idea. I think I’ll do the same.”

A Haddock tells Cuthbert he’s acting the calf
B Haddock says “We’ll all have a good laugh!”
C Bianca Castafiore asks Cuthbert if he has a wife

4 “Who is it? Did someone knock?”

A A milk van mysteriously blows up
B One of the seven crystal balls smashes
C An exploding bomb blows Cuthbert through his bedroom wall while still in bed

5 “Chicken-pox?”

A Jolyon Wagg asks Cuthbert to sign in the box
B Haddock calls Cuthbert a “jack-in-a-box!”
C General Alcazar calls him a sly old fox

6 “Rangoon? You must be joking?”

A Haddock exclaims, “ten thousand thundering typhoons!”
B Haddock calls Cuthbert a baboon
C Frank Wolff tells Cuthbert his rocket is ready to take off for the Moon

7 “Don’t be afraid. An eclipse, that’s all it is.”

A Professor Hercules hears what sounds like a shot outside
B Mr Carreidas asks Cuthbert if he enjoys battleships
C Haddock cries, “An eclipse! An eclipse! An eclipse!”

Feather Head-dress

In America, Tintin meets the Blackfeet people. These American Indians wear head-dresses made of feathers. Each feather shows how brave and fierce the person is. In this project, you can make your own superb head-dress.

Fearsome Feathers

Next time you go to a craft shop, look out for feathers that you could use to decorate your head-dress – choose large and small ones.

You will need:

- corrugated cardboard
- white paper
- 4 lengths of string, 15–20cm long
- colourful beads
- feathers
- pasta tubes
- felt-tip pens
- elastic
- pegs
- scissors
- glue

1 Cut the corrugated cardboard into a strip about 4cm x 25cm. Next, cut two discs 6cm across. Glue the white paper to the cardboard strip and decorate with felt-tip pens. (Look at the Chief's hat for ideas.)

2 Glue the two circles of white paper to the cardboard discs and decorate with the felt-tip pens. The Chief's discs are red but you can experiment with your own patterns.

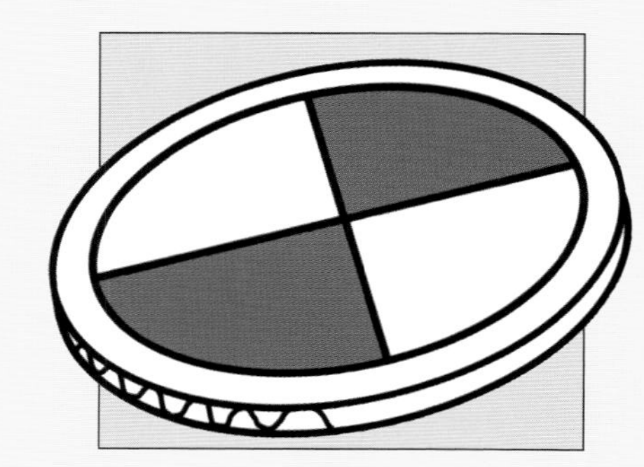

The Chief wears a head-dress made of eagle feathers.

3 Thread beads on to the lengths of string and knot one end of each.

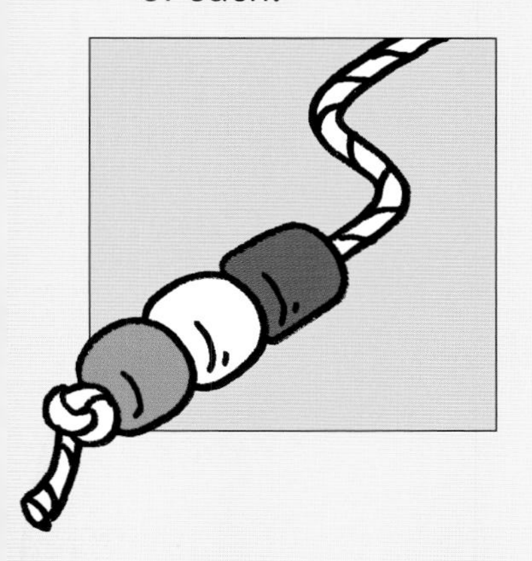

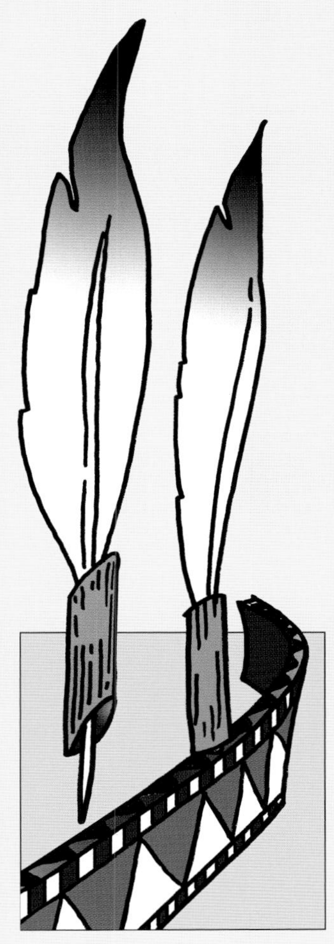

Special Meaning

Chiefs were not given a feather head-dress like a king is given a crown. Native warriors earned a feather with each brave act they did. So the Chief earned every single feather through brave acts.

4 Dip one of the feather stalks in the glue and use it to push the ends of the string up into the corrugated cardboard discs. Ask a grown-up for help!

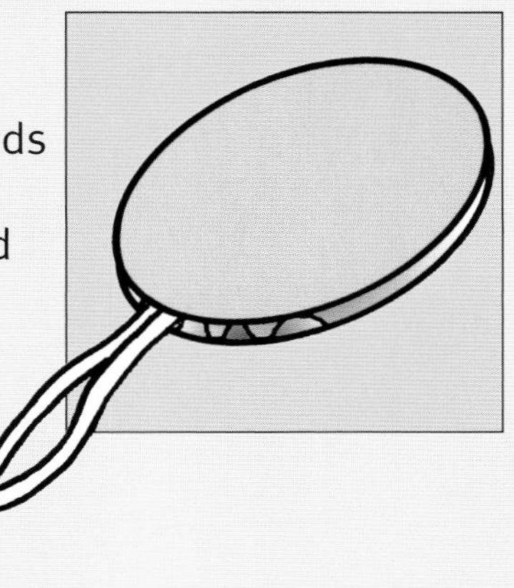

5 Thread the pasta tubes through each feather and push the ends into the strip of cardboard. Place large feathers in the middle and smaller ones each side.

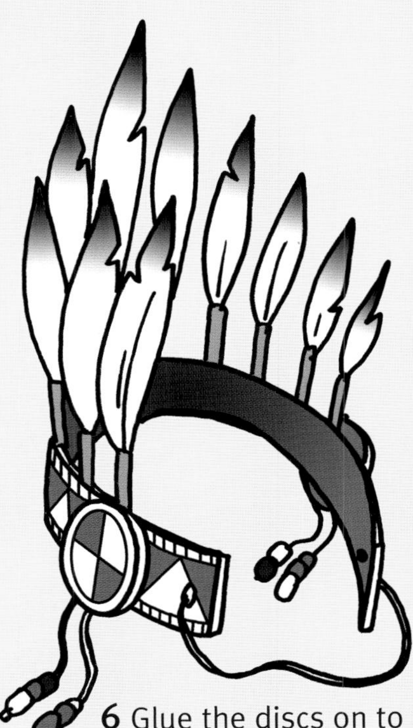

You will feel like a brave native chief when you wear your feather head-dress.

6 Glue the discs on to the sides and use pegs to hold them together until the glue has dried. Make a hole at each end of the strip and thread through elastic. Knot each end.

Great Inventions

When Tintin and Haddock first met Cuthbert Calculus, he was a poor, struggling inventor. All that changed with the success of his shark sub. Cuthbert sold the patent for a fortune, enabling him to let his inventive mind run wild!

Fizzical Science!

Cuthbert's house, as seen in *Red Rackham's Treasure*, looks like a mad scientist's laboratory. Among the weird inventions is his device for putting the bubbles in fizzy water.

To the Moon

To a scientist as original as Cuthbert, the sky's the limit. But with the invention of his space rocket, the Professor went even further – to the Moon and back! He thought of everything you would need in space, including spacesuits with breathing apparatus – even a special one for Snowy!

Undercover Bed

With so many curious creations taking up the space in his house, Cuthbert even invented a space-saving bed for himself.

Brush with Danger

This strange contraption gives your trousers a stiff brushing before they come out good as new. Just don't try it with your clothes still on!

Other Inventions

Here's a few other clever ideas the Professor has had:

- Magnetic space boots to help people avoid floating around in zero-gravity
- Herbal tablets to stop people drinking too much alcohol
- A new breed of white rose, named "Bianca" (for Bianca Castafiore)

Shark Submarine

Cuthbert made his fortune with his shark-shaped submarine. The sub shot to fame when Tintin used it to search for Red Rackham's treasure.

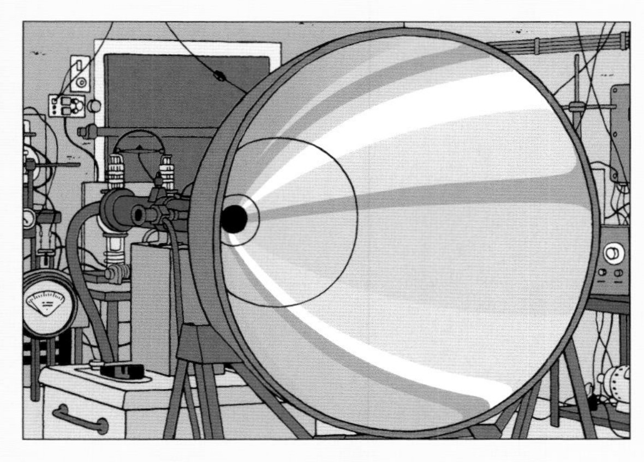

Deadly Weapon

Sometimes the Professor's inventions get him into trouble. When he invented an ultrasound emitter, he was kidnapped by people who wanted to use the device as a weapon.

Great Skates!

These motorised rollerskates are Cuthbert's answer to traffic jams. The cables are for steering.

Colour Television

Calculus invented colour television – using his "Super-Calcacolour". Unfortunately, the results caused headaches!

Call the Doctor !

Tintin is locked in a life-or-death struggle with evil Dr Müller in his country house. Study the picture carefully for 30 seconds, then turn the page upside down and cover the picture. Now answer the questions – how much can you remember ?

(Answers on page 68)

Questions

1 *What is in the picture that hangs above the fireplace ?*

2 *What are on the shelves ?*

3 *Name two things that have fallen on to the floor.*

4 *What is in the picture that hangs above the door ?*

5 *What type of hat is the man in the doorway wearing ?*

6 *What kind of lights are on the wall above the fireplace ?*

7 *What colour is Dr Müller's tie?*

8 *Name two objects on the desk in the foreground.*

Draw a Jeep

Follow these simple steps to draw the jeep that Thomson and Thompson drive so expertly in *Land of Black Gold*. Use a pencil at first and make light strokes. Then, if you make a mistake, you will be able to rub it out easily.

1 Draw a baseline for the wheels to sit on. If you use a ruler and protractor, the line should be -4 degrees. You could always trace steps 1 and 2.

2 Draw two ovals so that the baseline goes through their middles. Make sure they are centred, by drawing a guide line parallel to the baseline. Take care to get these first steps correct.

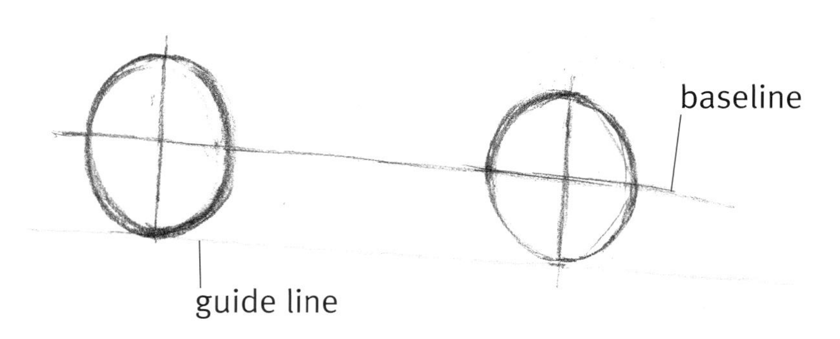

3 Think of the jeep's chassis (mainframe) as a box. Start with a rectangle. Sketch in the wheel hubs slightly off-centre.

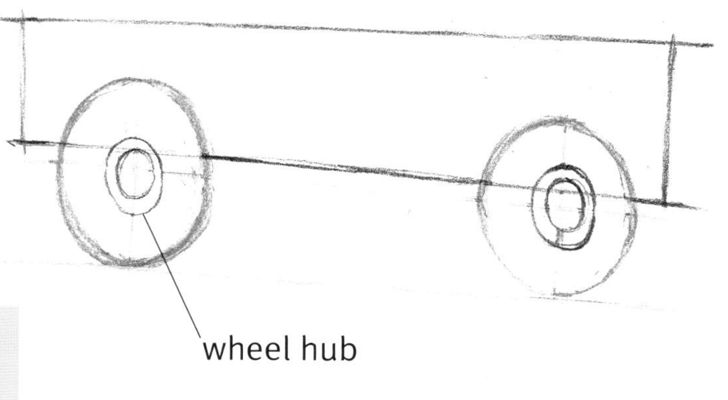

Angled Wheels

Here's how to draw realistic-looking wheels at an angle.

1 Sketch a cross and draw an oval around it. Then draw part of a same-size oval to its left and use a ruler to connect them at the top and bottom.

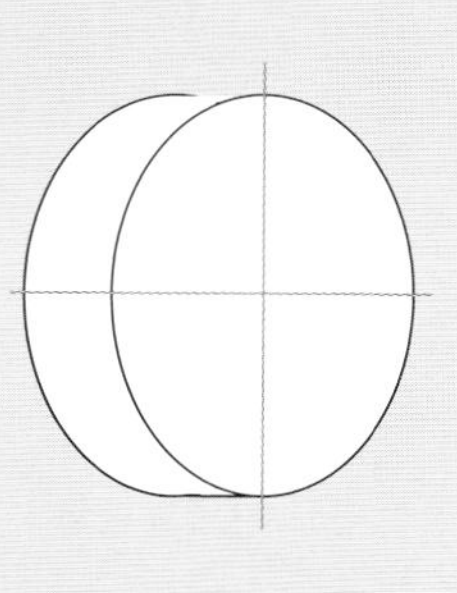

2 Now add a smaller oval a bit to its right, and an even smaller one just to the left.

4 Draw the top and front of the box to complete the chassis. Do the same with the wheels. Draw in the other wheels.

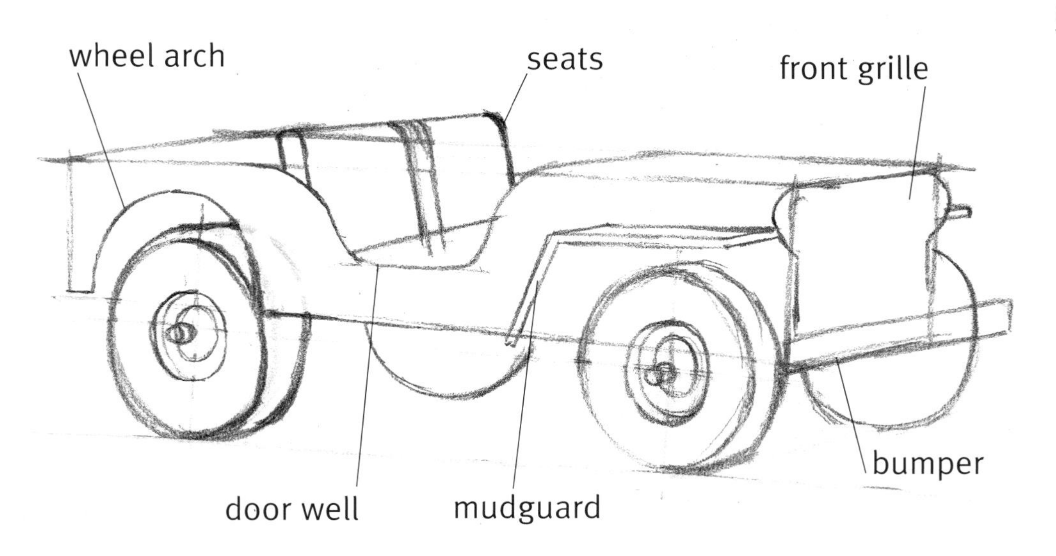

5 Now you must shape the rectangle to include the wheel arches, door well, seats and mudguards. Shape the front grille and add a bumper.

Here's a great trick! Reflect your drawing in a mirror to see it at different angles.

6 Add the final details, such as the steering wheel, windscreen, lights and number plate. Remember the brackets and fixings. Weld marks and joints make the drawing look extra-realistic, just like Hergé's drawings.

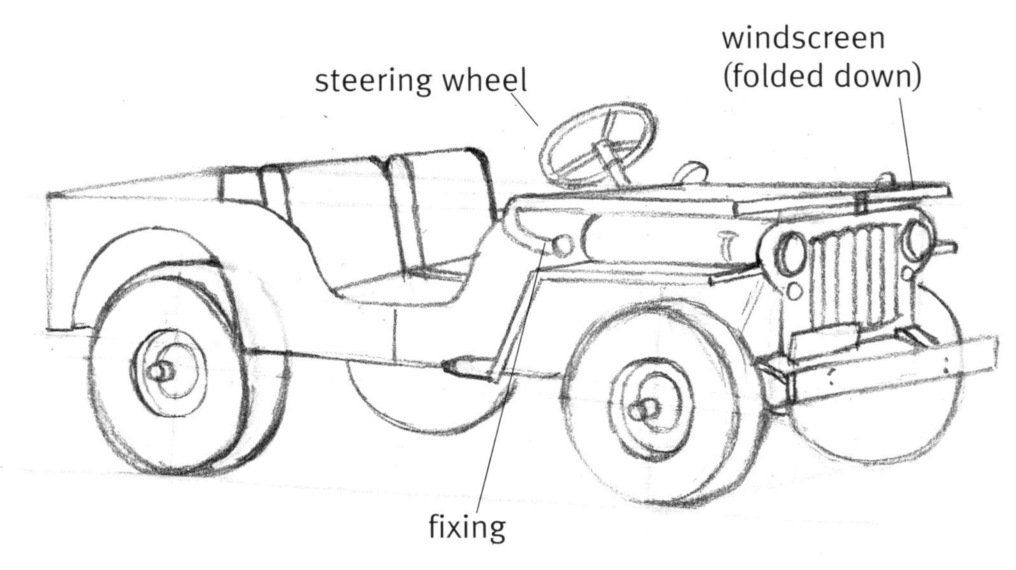

7 Here's how the finished drawing looks (see page 56 for how to draw Thomson and Thompson). Add the luggage and spare wheel. To make the image look like it's moving, you could add 'speed lines' and clouds of dust.

When you are happy with your sketch, colour it in and send the detectives off across the desert!

Answers

The Tintin Test
(pages 14–15)

Part 1: Marlinspike Hall
1. **B** 2. **A** 3. **C** 4. **B**

Part 2: Transport
1. **A** 2. **A** 3. **B** (*Explorers on the Moon* and *The Calculus Affair*)

Part 3: Great Escapes
1. **B** 2. **C** 3. **B**

Part 4: Tintin's Adventures
1. **C** 2. **B** 3. **C** 4. **B**

Unmask Tintin
(page 16)

Tintin is **G**.
(Mr Snowball is **A**,
Mrs Snowball is **B**,
the Colonel is **C**,
the Fakir is **D**,
the Maharaja's secretary is **E**,
the Japanese man is **F**.)

Fakir Word Search
(page 17)

C	S	C	A	I	R	O	E	T	B	U
M	I	L	S	N	O	W	Y	O	R	I
B	P	G	F	F	P	O	I	S	O	N
V	H	P	A	K	K	R	G	J	T	G
A	A	Y	T	R	L	M	C	Y	H	S
S	R	T	F	H	S	E	C	R	E	T
D	A	G	C	T	J	L	Y	G	R	T
P	O	I	K	I	H	O	S	K	H	U
R	H	E	U	N	P	K	E	B	O	R
S	O	F	E	T	S	H	S	R	O	L
D	F	A	K	I	R	L	E	J	D	L
I	M	L	U	N	F	D	A	R	T	R
P	M	A	D	N	E	S	S	N	M	C

Morse Mystery
(pages 18–19)

The message reads:
emergency. captain haddock is on a secret mission

Seeing Spots
(page 24)

Ayesha is at the end of rope **C**.

Mirror Muddle
(page 25)

The correct order is 6, 4, 2, 9, 8, 3, 7, 5, 1.

Bird Brains
(pages 34–35)

1. penguin
2. swan
3. parrot
4. magpie
5. owl
6. condor
7. seagull

Daring Escape
(pages 38–39)

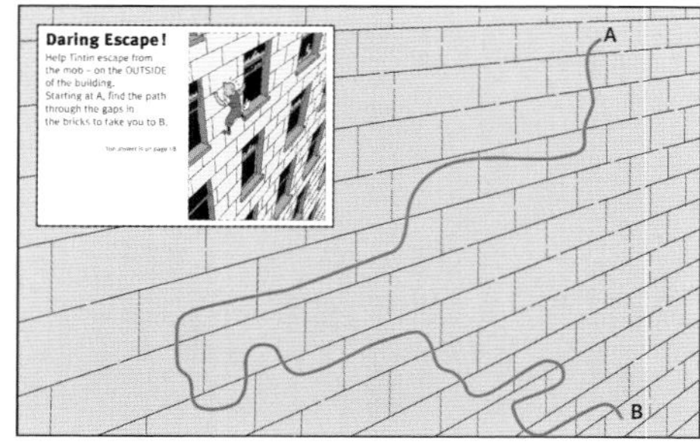

Memorable Journey
(pages 42–43)

Tintin's journey ends at **D**.

Up-close and Personal
(pages 44–45)

1. Bianca Castafiore
2. Captain Haddock
3. Nestor
4. Tintin
5. Thompson
6. Snowy
7. Cuthbert Calculus
8. Thomson

Pardon?
(pages 58–59)

1. **C** (*The Castafiore Emerald*)
2. **B** (*Red Rackham's Treasure*)
3. **B** (*Tintin and the Picaros*)
4. **C** (*Destination Moon*)
5. **B** (*The Calculus Affair*)
6. **A** (*Flight 714 to Sydney*)
7. **C** (*Prisoners of the Sun*)

Call The Doctor!
(pages 64–65)

1. A ship
2. Books
3. Telephone, cigarettes, ashtray, sidetables
4. Horse and rider
5. A cap
6. Candles
7. Green
8. Pot, paper, pen tray

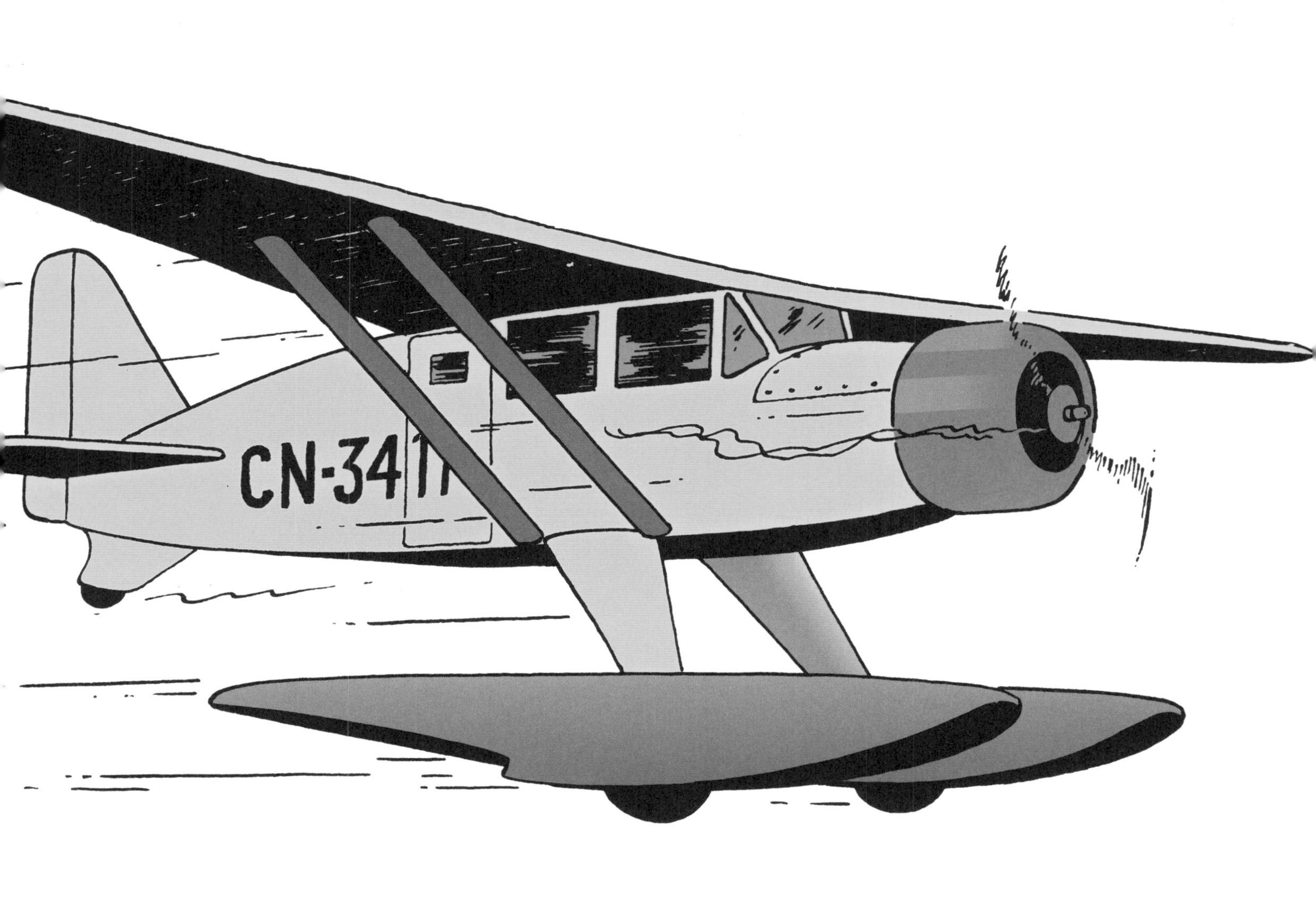
CN-34